VANCOUVER

The Art *of* LIVING WELL

▲ RON WATTS / FIRST LIGHT PHOTOGRAPHY

By P ETER C. N EWMAN

and A LEX W ATERHOUSE - H AYWARD

VANCOUVER

The Art *of* LIVING WELL

Profiles in Excellence and Captions by EVE LAZARUS
Art Direction by BRIAN GROPPE
Sponsored by THE VANCOUVER BOARD OF TRADE

▲ © ALBERT NORMANDIN

© BOB AKESTER

Library of Congress Cataloging-in-Publication Data

Newman, Peter Charles.
       Vancouver : the art of living well / by Peter C. Newman and Alex
Waterhouse-Hayward ; profiles in excellence and captions by Eve
Lazarus.
              p.   cm. -- (Urban tapestry series)
       "Sponsored by the Vancouver Board of Trade."
       Includes index.
       ISBN 1-881096-34-3
       1. Vancouver (B.C.)--Civilization.   2. Vancouver (B.C.)--Pictorial
works.   3. Vancouver (B.C.)--Economic conditions.   4. Industries-
-British Columbia--Vancouver.   I. Waterhouse-Hayward, Alex, 1943-
II. Lazarus, Eve, 1959-   . III. Vancouver Board of Trade.
IV.   Title. V.   Series.
F1089.5.V22N49   1996
971.1'33--dc20

96-32967
CIP

Towery Publishing, Inc., 1835 Union Avenue, Memphis, TN 38104

Publisher: J. ROBERT TOWERY
Executive Publisher: JENNY MCDOWELL
National Sales Manager: STEPHEN HUNG
Regional Sales Manager: MICHELE SYLVESTRO
National Marketing Director: ELEANOR D. CAREY
Marketing Coordinator: CAROL CULPEPPER
Project Director: ROBERT ZALAUDEK

Executive Editor: DAVID B. DAWSON
Senior Editor: MICHAEL C. JAMES
Profiles Manager/Associate Editor: MARY JANE ADAMS
Associate Editors: LORI BOND, LYNN CONLEE, CARLISLE HACKER

Profile Designers: JENNIFER BAUGHER, LAURIE LEWIS, ANN WARD
Technical Director: WILLIAM H. TOWERY
Production Manager: BRENDA PATTAT
Production Assistant: JEFF MCDONALD

URBAN
TAPESTRY
SERIES
TOWERY
PUBLISHING, INC.

By Peter C. Newman

Vancouver: The Art of Living Well

"VANCOUVER SITS INSIDE THE BOWL OF SUCH A heavenly hunk of geography that no matter how people spend their lives in and around Canada's third-largest city, they can never escape the feeling of having been granted the mandate of heaven."

By Eve Lazarus

Profiles in Excellence

A LOOK AT THE CORPORATIONS, BUSINESSES, professional groups, and community service organizations that have made this book possible.

Photographers

235

Index of Profiles

239

Vancouver: The Art of Living Well
By Peter C. Newman

THE ESSENCE OF A GREAT CITY CAN BE CAUGHT in a phrase. To me, the definitive comment about Vancouver was the answer given by Christopher Newton—the well-known Canadian director/producer who now runs the Shaw Festival near Toronto—in response to my question about whether the Pacific city was a good place for live theatre.

He shook his head and said that no, it wasn't, although he had spent a decade on Canada's west coast staging experimental plays and still has a home here.

"Vancouver makes for lousy theatre," he emphasized. "No matter what you do, you're always competing with God."

Newton had a point, and not just about theatre.

Vancouver sits inside the bowl of such a heavenly hunk of geography that no matter how people spend their lives in and around Canada's third-largest city, they can never escape the feeling of having been granted the mandate of heaven. That euphoric sense of place has much to do with two natural features: the Coast Mountains that rise up like jagged green battlements, providing the city's glorious sightlines, and the Pacific Ocean, a horizontal balance to the mountains' vertical thrust and a daily stage show that contrasts with the mountains' perpetuity. The tides, which flood and ebb past greater Vancouver's many beaches, and the dozen bridges make its citizens feel as if they were islanders. As islanders of the mind, Vancouverites tend to be more aware of the sights, sounds, and scents around them—living in harmony with the turning of the seasons, the faring of the tides, and the grace notes of the sunsets.

Vancouver's charm isn't all the work of a benign deity; much of the credit belongs to municipal planners who have not allowed any freeways to scar the cityscape. Because its core lacks a central highway system, the city's neighborhoods have largely escaped the blight of urban sprawl and strip malls. Despite Vancouver's relatively elegant traffic patterns, its downtown area is crammed into a narrow peninsula that gives it the most geographically constrained landmass of any major city in North America. Beyond that core, however, there's a lot more room to breathe. To the north the coastal highway disappears into dirt tracks just past Powell River. To the west lies Vancouver Island and, beyond that, nothing but ocean until you hit the beaches of Hokkaido in northern Japan. To the east are the untouchable farms of the Fraser Valley and the Lillooet Range, which blocks expansion at Hope. To the south is another country, beginning with Washington State and expanding, via Interstate 5, all the way down to Tijuana.

If you drive north on almost any downtown artery, you'll find that beyond street's end lies an anchored freighter, a bold reminder of Vancouver's unique

relationship to the Pacific. Early morning sea gulls wheel over the city, mewing their salutes to the dawn. Vancouver possesses the physical beauty of Rio de Janeiro or Hong Kong, without the crowds.

But it's much more than that. Vancouver is less a city than a destination. This is Canada's psychological and geographical frontier, the end of the line—as far as you can run and still have Medicare. Like most frontier people who live on the edge, Vancouverites operate according to their own rules and consider themselves as much citizens of their time as of their place.

The arts and commerce flourish side by side in Vancouver, and both seem to blend in with the city's natural beauty rather than compete with it. For a couple of months each summer, Vancouver's majestic cityscape and mountains form a backdrop for Bard on the Beach (ABOVE), an event during which ever-popular Shakespearean plays are performed in the outdoor setting of Vanier Park.

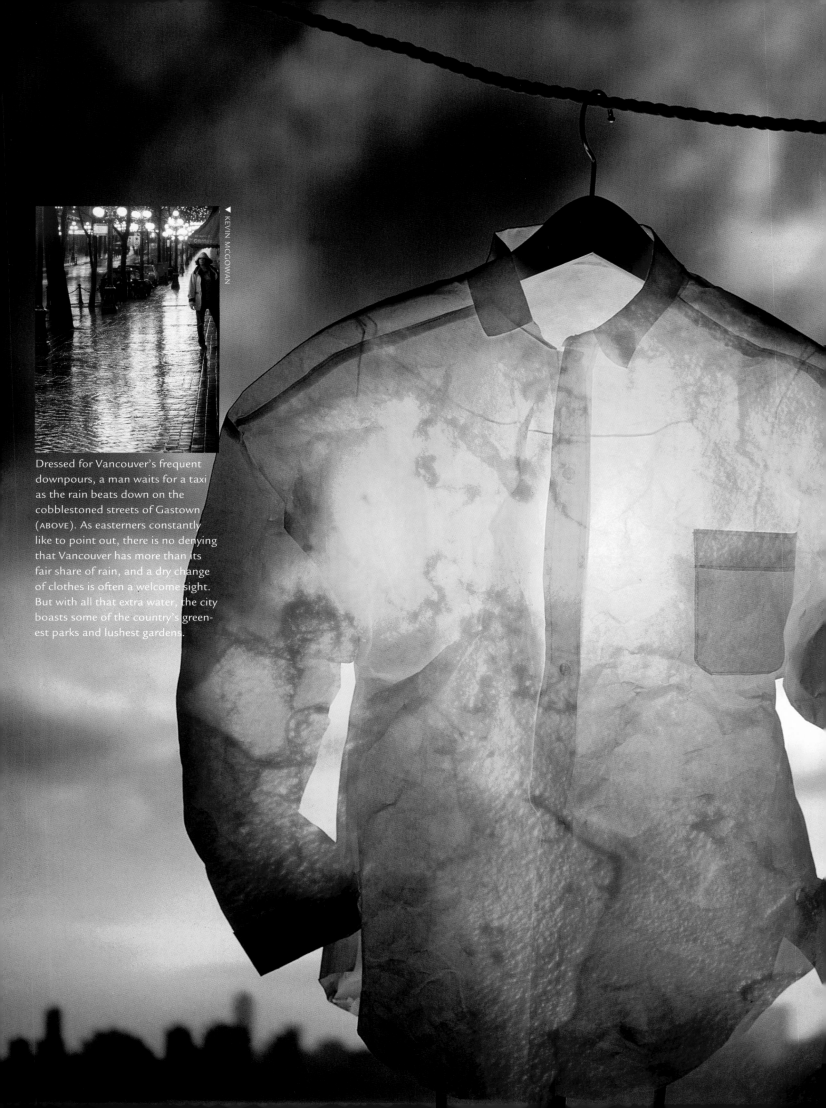

Dressed for Vancouver's frequent downpours, a man waits for a taxi as the rain beats down on the cobblestoned streets of Gastown (ABOVE). As easterners constantly like to point out, there is no denying that Vancouver has more than its fair share of rain, and a dry change of clothes is often a welcome sight. But with all that extra water, the city boasts some of the country's greenest parks and lushest gardens.

DESPITE NEWTON'S WARNING ABOUT COMPET-
ing with the Almighty, life in Vancouver is actually more theatrical than real.
After all, there's not much satisfaction in playing your conventional self when
you have such a magnificent backdrop. Vancouver people tend to live for
the moment, playing out whatever role they assign themselves, with little

regard for history or tradition. The city was named after Captain George Vancouver, the British explorer who landed here in 1792. It was established as an afterthought by the Canadian Pacific Railway, which originally picked nearby Port Moody as its western terminus but moved shop in 1886. Vancouver's history is so brief, in fact, that some of its senior citizens still remember their fathers telling them tales of how they were chased down the main thoroughfare (what is now Granville Street) by wild bears. When a city is only two generations of memories old, anyone who arrived more than two flights ago can become a founding father.

Having once had a deserved reputation as the favorite home port of Canadian hippies— back in the 1960s Vancouver's Kitsilano district was known as Canada's Haight-Ashbury—the city still reflects that legacy in its New Age sensibilities and habits. Vancouverites collect and occasionally read holistic self-help books; frequently eat out at "energy bars" such as O-Tooz; dress for comfort instead of fashion; place spiritual quests above material comforts; and, above all, share an intense preoccupation with protecting the environment. The eco-activists, Pan-flutists, skateboarders, and street chess champions who gather at Robson Square represent the city as eloquently as the Howe Street stock promoters whose flinty eyes conjure images of baccarat dealers. So do the

Stanley Park sea-wall joggers who appear to be bobbing through a technicolor aquarium, the introspective worshippers living out their ch'i at Sun Yat-Sen Gardens, and the postgraduate yuppies of Kerrisdale and Kitsilano whose lives are measured out in coffee grains.

The city runs on two equally essential fluids: coffee and rain. In Vancouver the biblical designation B.C. stands for "Before Coffee," the years before 1992, when the first Starbucks outlets appeared in the city and drinking refined java became an art form. The Seattle-based chain now has franchise outlets on most busy street corners, with two—plus a third no-name coffee house—at a particularly frantic intersection on Robson Street. Few serious conversations take place in Vancouver without the steamy hiss of espresso machines in the background. Choosing between sprinkles of chocolate or cinnamon on your latte-to-stay ("double short, low fat, easy on the foam") ranks ahead of reciting the Lord's Prayer as a daily ritual.

The rain—the never-ending rain—is another matter altogether. Contrary to local mythology, downpours really *are* so frequent that you expect to grow webbed feet. The showers seem to materialize out of nowhere, with none of the usual meteorological warnings—no storm clouds or wind gales; it just rains. No matter how often some cheerful

type explains that it's all part of enjoying Vancouver's Mediterranean-like climate, the fact remains that the liquified air yields 55 inches of rain per year. In 1966 it even rained for 60 consecutive days and nights, which everyone agreed was unusual.

But there are compensations. Despite all the rain, Vancouver entertains nearly 7 million tourists each year, who leave behind $2 billion. And as the good folks at Tourism Vancouver like to boast, the city's winter climate is so mild that crocuses greet the sun by mid-February and visitors can ski and sail or catch a spring salmon, all in the space of 30 minutes. "That's only true," *Vancouver Sun* columnist Denny Boyd has pointed out, "as long as your skis have quick release bindings. Otherwise, it might take up to 45 minutes."

People in Vancouver shine both before and behind the camera. Filmmaker and director Mina Shum, pictured above, received rave reviews for her film *Double Happiness* and is an important part of the city's thriving movie industry.

VANCOUVER HAS A GREAT DEAL MORE TO OFFER than beautiful scenery, interesting people, and ample doses of coffee and rain. Sports and entertainment options are now presented in some of the newest and flashiest facilities on the continent. The NHL Canucks and NBA Grizzlies share the new $160 million General Motors Place,

an impressive venue that seats 20,000 and boasts a concert-hall-quality sound system. Nearby, the Ford Centre for the Performing Arts opened its doors with a critically acclaimed revival of *Show Boat*. Another addition to the cultural scene is the striking $100 million public library, which has been designed to resemble Rome's ancient Coliseum.

In most cities, great houses inspire great parties. But some say it's the other way around in Vancouver, where many a dwelling was first mapped on a cocktail napkin. No matter the origin, the best local architecture attempts to incorporate the sky and the sea—two of Vancouver's greatest attributes.

Examples of fine architecture fill the city's neighborhoods. Southwest Marine Drive is the most prestigious address, but the rhododendrons of old Shaughnessy still hide the most imposing homes. (A mansion on Osler Avenue changed hands for $7 million in the autumn of 1995.) The cliff dwellers of Caulfeild, Whytecliff, and Gleneagles enjoy the most exciting views. The golf clubs of choice are the Capilano and

Shaughnessy, where initiation fees run to $50,000; the Royal Vancouver Yacht Club has the best facilities and no waiting list.

Good restaurants abound as well. My personal favorites are The Ivy on Fourth Avenue, which serves the best roast duck in the universe, and The Cannery, which is impossible to beat for great seafood. They are but a couple of the fine eateries you'll find in Vancouver.

Living in greater Vancouver is easy, but it's not free. Most of the city's nearly 2 million citizens are convinced—and rightly so—that they inhabit a field of dreams: If they build well, the opportunities will come. Opportunities do exist in Vancouver, and most doors are open. There still endures a powerful rearguard establishment whose members can trace their bloodlines to the original forestry and mining fortunes that opened up Canada's west coast, but most of the active players belong to a new generation—self-made and classless. Unlike the more settled and rigid hierarchies of Canada's great eastern cities, Vancouver welcomes the muscle and talent of

newcomers. Despite rumors to the contrary, the cost of making it in Vancouver is as high as it is anywhere: Success comes right out of the marrow. Even if the city's working population spends an inordinate amount of time jogging, sailing, skiing, hiking, and playing at every conceivable sport except bull fighting, it's usually in training for more "professional" pursuits. Prime time is still work time in Vancouver.

General Motors Place (ABOVE), home to the Vancouver Canucks and Grizzlies, opened in 1995, the same year that the coliseumlike Vancouver Public Library (OPPOSITE) gave the city an airy structure for its more serious cultural pursuits.

Vancouver's history, though short, is intrinsically tied to its relationship with the water. The city's port handles more than 70 million tonnes of cargo, shipping containers, and bulk shipments of coal, grain, potash, and sulphur each year, as well as lumber and wood pulp that is worth about $40 billion. The total tonnage handled in Vancouver is about the same as for the ports of Montreal, Halifax, St. John's, and Quebec combined.

CONSIDER THIS: VANCOUVER HOUSES ABOUT 180 major corporations with total revenues of more than $65 billion. Once on the commercial margin of North America, this city by the sea is becoming recognized as a strategically located nexus of international commerce. Midway—in terms of distances and time zones—

between New York and Tokyo, Vancouver is beginning to think of itself in a radically different

way. Instead of limiting their self-image to being citizens of the largest city on Canada's *western* shore—part of the country but only on its outer economic margin—the new generation of globally minded Vancouver businesspeople realize they inhabit the ideally located 21st-century trading post on the *eastern* coast of the Pacific Ocean.

That's partly a matter of proximity: Vancouver is 350 miles closer to Tokyo than it is to Halifax, on Canada's Atlantic shore. The significance of this

shift in perception is hard to exaggerate. Most economists agree that the world's economic future will be decided in Asia and that Vancouver will be the essential gateway to that "tomorrow country."

Vancouver already exports more than a quarter of its gross municipal product, which totals more than twice the national average. The city's main economic function has always been that of an entrepôt, a transfer point between interior producers and overseas consumers. That traffic moves mainly through Vancouver's magnificent harbor, which has become North America's third-largest port. Ever since the first departure of the Australia-bound timber ship *Ellen Lewis* in 1864, the city has been serving world trade routes, which currently extend to 92 countries. It is highly symbolic that most of Vancouver's downtown buildings face Burrard Inlet, which provides the basin for one of the world's best-protected natural harbors. The city's economy has always responded to faraway events: the Canadian Confederation in 1867; the gold rushes of the late

1800s; the building of the Panama Canal in 1914; the two world wars; the Canadian mining and oil boom of the 1950s; the great Chinese wheat sales of the 1960s; and, more recently, economic globalization and the rise of southeast Asia.

As business on an international scale takes over an even greater share of the overall economy, air transportation will become increasingly important. Vancouver is ready. The city's privately run airport has just completed a $300 million-plus expansion that will eventually double its annual capacity of 10 million passengers. Vancouver leads in several other modes of transport: Its Sea Bus, linking downtown with the north shore across Burrard Inlet, is the only one of its kind; Sky Train, the city's elevated, automated light rapid transit system, was the first of its kind to be installed anywhere; and the Royal Hudson, which takes passengers up scenic Howe Sound to Squamish, is the only scheduled mainline steam locomotive service remaining in North America.

Vancouver's harbor, rail, and air links have helped position the city as North America's gateway to the world. More than 300,000 jets take off and land at the Vancouver International Airport every year.

THE REALIZATION OF VANCOUVER'S ECONOMIC destiny will require some fundamental changes in its citizens' attitudes. A few years ago, the American futurist Herman Kahn was hired to draw up his vision of Vancouver's outlook. He promptly dubbed the city "the Paris of the North" and predicted that the Fraser Valley was capable

▼ ROB KRUYT

of accommodating about 10 million people at low densities "with possibilities for growth that are almost unlimited. . . . Vancouver people really put quality of life far ahead of economic growth," a trait, he added, that "overwhelmingly amazes me."

More recent computer-generated projections call for the arrival of 1.2 million newcomers by 2021. Meanwhile, nearly 100,000 people are moving into greater Vancouver annually, some 35,000 from other parts of Canada and approximately 65,000 from overseas, mainly the Orient. The influx, mainly from Hong Kong, Taiwan, Japan, and Singapore, started on a large scale after the Expo '86 world's Fair introduced Vancouver's potential to international investors, and China first began to make the noises culminating in its 1997 takeover of Hong Kong. Asian immigrants have been arriving on Canada's Pacific shores ever since, so that at least one in four Vancouverites is now of Asian descent. That makes the city the most Asian-flavored community on the continent. Futurist John Naisbitt summed up the trend most succinctly when he concluded, "Vancouver is becoming world headquarters of the overseas Chinese."

These dynamic arrivals have caught the Vancouver spirit. They've quickly learned what longtime Vancouverites have always known: Competing with God can be a whole lot of fun—and mighty profitable.

MOUNT SEYMOUR IS ONE OF three North Shore mountains that attract downhill and cross-country ski enthusiasts in the winter, and hikers, mountain bikers, and sightseers in the warmer months.

PAGES 18 AND 19: © 1996 STEFAN SCHULHOF

IT TAKES AN ADVENTUROUS climber to challenge the Teflon-coated sails of Canada Place, but this maintenance worker is rewarded with a spectacular aerial view of downtown Vancouver, including the air-inflated roof of B.C. Place Stadium, Burrard Inlet, and the North Shore mountains.

KNOWN AS YVR, THE VANCOUVER International Airport holds a fascination for people of all ages. The two red cedar *Welcome Figures* greet passengers to the new international terminal, the first in North America to be built specifically for connecting passengers.

URBAN DWELLERS WHO PREFER to see stunt work in the air can occasionally get a glimpse of the Canadian Snowbirds—in this case, as they fly over the Pan Pacific Hotel in downtown Vancouver (OPPOSITE, TOP RIGHT). In a similar display, the Ray-Ban Specials undertake hair-raising manoeuvres through The Lions (ABOVE).

BURRARD INLET IS VANCOUVER'S second-busiest airport, with more than 60,000 takeoffs and landings occurring every year amid sailboats, cruise ships, and other floating obstacles.

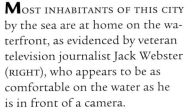

▲ ALEX WATERHOUSE-HAYWARD

MOST INHABITANTS OF THIS CITY by the sea are at home on the waterfront, as evidenced by veteran television journalist Jack Webster (RIGHT), who appears to be as comfortable on the water as he is in front of a camera.

The Seabus that crosses the Burrard Inlet from Vancouver to North Vancouver every 15 minutes is an integral part of the Lower Mainland's transportation system (BOTTOM LEFT).

The cruise ship *Regent Star*, docked at a North Vancouver shipyard, waits to take its next load of passengers to their destination (TOP LEFT). Carrying more than 600,000 travellers each year to Alaska, the cruise ship industry leaves behind more than $130 million in economic benefits for Vancouver.

WHEN CAPTAIN GEORGE Vancouver sailed through the Burrard Inlet in 1792, he was the first European to enter the region. Even though he only spent one night, it was enough to have the city named after him and gain him a permanent place outside City Hall.

SCULPTED IN 1936, *The Rocket* welcomed visitors to the Vancouver International Airport. This replica, located near the Cambie Street Bridge, was constructed by Sheet Metal Workers' Union Local 280 for the city's centennial in 1986.

EO. GIBSON   ALD. GRIFFITHS   ALD. BALFOUR   ALD. DUNN   J.J. BLAKE   ALD. HUMPHRIES   G.F. BALDWIN   DR. McGUIGAN
                                                          CITY SOLICITOR   CITY TREASURER
CITY HALL & 1st COUNCIL, 1886.
      ALD. COLDWELL ALD. HAMILTON ALD. NORTHCOTT   MAYOR McLEAN   ALD. HAMILTON ALD. CORDINER   T.F. McGUIGAN

THROUGHOUT VANCOUVER'S history, City Hall, in all its forms, has kept a paternal eye on the growing community. Three of the diverse city councillors who watch over Vancouver today are (OPPOSITE, FROM LEFT) Gordon Price, Sam Sullivan, and Jenny Kwan.

OVER THE PAST 20 YEARS THE shores of False Creek have evolved from an industrial eyesore to a trendy community of high-density residential housing favored by both recreational boaters and fishermen.

GRANVILLE ISLAND HAS UNDERgone its own metamorphosis. In 1957 it was the site of several sawmills and other heavy industry (TOP), but, almost 40 years later, the island is far more famous for its public market and pottery (BOTTOM).

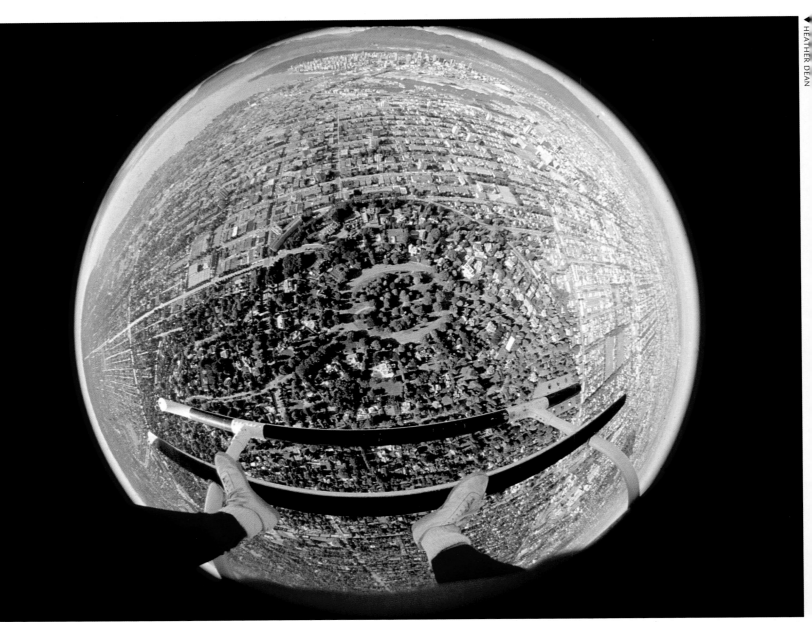

SHAUGHNESSY, AN EXCLUSIVE Vancouver neighborhood, is uniquely captured by local photographer Heather Dean. Dangling from a helicopter, Dean uses a fish-eye lens to perfectly mimick the circular street.

A BIRD'S-EYE VIEW OF SOUTHWEST Marine Drive (LEFT) offers an unusual perspective on one of the city's impressive mansions. The historic Mount Pleasant area is one of Vancouver's oldest neighborhoods (RIGHT).

VANCOUVER IS MADE UP OF
dozens of neighborhoods, each
with its own unique characteris-
tics and identity. The city's history is reflected in its beautiful
heritage houses.

WHILE CLOSE TO THE CORE OF Gastown, Abbot Street remains part of a traditional neighborhood where its residents tolerate the invasion of nearby tourism.

PATTERNS OF LIGHT AND SHADOW add their own flourish to Vancouver's architectural details.

BUILT IN 1969, THE AWARD-winning West Coast Transmission Building was an architectural marvel of its time. Most of the weight of the high-rise structure is borne by cables suspended from a central point on the roof.

No OTHER ARCHITECT HAS HIS stamp placed so firmly on the city as Arthur Erickson (BOTTOM LEFT). When Erickson-designed Simon Fraser University opened its mountaintop campus in 1965, it was a stunning feat of modernity (TOP). Some 11 years later, the cliff-hugging Museum of Anthropology brought to life another award-winning Erickson design (BOTTOM RIGHT).

The city's old courthouse on Robson, designed by Francis Rattenbury in 1907, was remodelled in 1983 by Erickson to house the Vancouver Art Gallery (OPPOSITE).

A CONTROVERSIAL PIECE OF architecture when it opened in 1995, the Vancouver Public Library feeds the mind *and* the senses. Unlike a traditional library, it is a noisy spacious building, with circular seating areas on every other level and reading arcades on each of its seven floors.

Culture is relative in Vancouver. It can be found in unexpected places, whether you're roller-blading down the steps of the Vancouver Art Gallery, tucked away in the Vancouver Public Library, or playing chess in Robson Square.

◄ ROGER BROOKS   ► DOANE GREGORY

IT TAKES A HEAD FOR HEIGHTS and a resistance to vertigo to look down from the CIBC building onto Burrard Street or from the top of a Lions Gate Bridge tower onto Stanley Park.

BUILT IN THE 1930S, THE MARINE Building (OPPOSITE) underwent a massive restoration in 1989. Its ornate art deco façade is a perfect setting for British Columbia's burgeoning motion picture in- dustry. Film crews are a common sight on the streets of Vancouver, and the call of "roll cameras" is now of just passing interest to locals.

THE ART OF LIVING WELL   55

WHEN PHOTOGRAPHER BRENDA Hemsing moved from Calgary to Vancouver, she became fascinated with the city's older buildings and its birds. Here, she shoots the Dominion Building on Hastings Street (ABOVE) and the Hotel Europe Building in Gastown (OP-POSITE). And no, birds *don't* fly differently in Vancouver: The buildings and the birds were photographed separately and double-exposed.

A LOCAL LANDMARK, THE "W" survived the 1993 demise of the 101-year-old Woodwards, a British Columbia-based family-owned department store.

Whether Vancouverites love or hate the city's unique architecture and public sculptures, they can always find a talking point. The futuristic geodesic dome (TOP) is known to locals as "The Golf Ball." Built at the Expo '86 preview centre at the head of False Creek, the structure now houses the city's popular Science World. Vancouver's statue of Atlas (BOTTOM), located outside Fitness World on Kingsway in Burnaby, is similar to its more famous New York City cousin.

NINE O'CLOCK IS AN IMPORTANT time in the city. The Nine O'Clock Gun, which originally sounded on Sunday evenings during fishing season to signal the end of the day of fishing, still discharges its blast from Stanley Park (BOTTOM LEFT AND RIGHT).

With Vancouver's rise to cultural prominence, the nine o'clock hour has taken on another meaning—theatre time. The $24.5 million Ford Centre for the Performing Arts now gives locals and tourists access to some of the world's finest theatrical productions (TOP).

► ROBERT KWONG

VANCOUVERITES CAN FIND MUSIC to suit all their tastes. Sergiu Comissiona, musical director for the Vancouver Symphony, pro-motes the *1812* Overture (ABOVE). Vancouver rock star Bryan Adams takes a walk by the Marine Building (OPPOSITE).

VANCOUVER'S BRIDGES ARE AN extension of its roads, and are relied upon for transportation as heavily as the water they span.

LOCATED AT THE TIP OF POINT Grey, the University of British Columbia has more than 31,000 students enrolled in graduate and postgraduate studies. Alumni include former prime ministers Kim Campbell and John Turner, wheel chair athlete Rick Hansen, and opera singer Judith Forst.

LOCAL ARTISTS OF ALL AGES HAVE
some of Canada's most vibrant
and beautiful scenery as inspiration. As a result, many colorful
scenes, like this Granville Island
mural (OPPOSITE), dot the city.

DEEPLY ENTRENCHED IN
Vancouver, Chinatown retains all
the complexities of the Orient.
The second-largest such neighborhood in North America, it is
steeped in tradition.

IN CHINATOWN, MANY INHABIT-ants shop in the traditional markets, while others farm their own produce.

If Vancouver is the grand gateway to the Pacific, then its neighbor Richmond is surely the unassuming doorway. City officials estimate more than 50,000 immigrants have moved to Richmond over the past two decades, about two-thirds of whom are from Hong Kong, Taiwan, and mainland China. Their widespread influence can be seen everywhere—in a shrine to Buddha in Richmond (BOTTOM LEFT), during a Chinese New Year celebration (TOP), or at the Aberdeen Centre, one of five Asian-style malls in the area (BOTTOM RIGHT).

▼ ADAM GIBBS

LYNN HEADWATERS REGIONAL
Park, a wilderness of magical
qualities on Vancouver's North
Shore, lends itself to many artistic
interpretations. Photographer
Brenda Hemsing used high-speed
surveillance film to capture these
woodsy scenes, and Ian Martin
completed the photogravure—a
printing process rarely seen today—for the mystical look.

STANLEY PARK, A 1,000-ACRE
(400-hectare) forest in the heart
of Vancouver, offers many attrac-
tions, including this hollow tree
through which visitors can drive
their cars.

ANYONE WHO HAPPENS BY THIS
downtown building at 745
Thurlow will discover an unexpected urban rain forest as depicted by Vancouver artists Terry
Gilecki and Robert Dobie.

IN AN INTERESTING TURN OF events, a pair of old tree trunks find new life as lumberjacks. Standing tall atop Grouse Mountain, these creations were carved almost entirely by chain saw. Artist Glen Greensides has been commissioned to create a total of 18 works as a tribute to the region's forests. Carvings reach a height of 25 feet and are crafted from salvaged stumps anywhere between 800 and 1,200 years old.

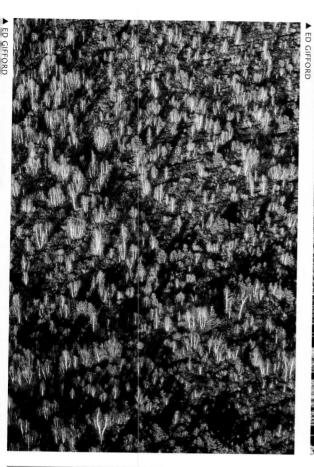

ED GIFFORD

ED GIFFORD

FORESTRY IS THE PROVINCE'S number one industry, creating thousands of jobs in the area and bringing many economic benefits. More than 7,500 metric tonnes of wood products were handled by the Port of Vancouver in 1995.

THE RIVERS AND MOUNTAINS OF British Columbia have helped make tourism the second-largest industry in the province. Even sockeye salmon make their way to the area, coming to spawn in the Adams River. The film and television industry is another frequent visitor, pouring more than $500 million into British Columbia's economy in 1995.

Every summer, the *Royal Hudson* steams along the coast of Howe Sound to Squamish, enthralling sightseers with its magnificent vistas, such as Whistler Village (PAGE 104) and Grouse Mountain (PAGE 105).

PAGE 104: GREG GRIFFITH / FIRST LIGHT PHOTOGRAPHY
PAGE 105: PETER TIMMERMANS

A. GRIFFITHS-BELT / FIRST LIGHT PHOTOGRAPHY

ACCESSIBLE ONLY BY WATER OR A long climb from the University Endowment Lands, Wreck Beach has developed a unique culture that attracts artists and free spirits from around the world.

MINUTES FROM THE CITY CENTRE, the West End is the most densely populated area of Vancouver, and one of the most beautiful. While the majority of West Enders live in high-rise apartment buildings, they are minutes from the Sea Wall at Stanley Park (RIGHT) and from the beaches of English Bay (OPPOSITE TOP), which have remained popular for decades. Tiko Kerr depicted English Bay in his 1993 painting *Spring Wind* (OPPOSITE BOTTOM).

VANCOUVER

Vancouver's scenery has inspired great artistic expression—from Emily Carr's 1931 painting *Tree Trunk* (LEFT) to more recent works by Tiko Kerr. In *Eugenia* (OPPOSITE), Kerr offers his interpretation of the Eugenia building, designed by Richard Henriques, whom Kerr has described as "one of the most poetic architects in the city."

NAT BAILEY IS ONE OF THOSE rags-to-riches stories that every city has in its business and cultural history. Having started out selling peanuts at baseball games, he founded the first White Spot restaurant in 1928, and two decades later, the city named a baseball stadium in his honor. The Nat Bailey Stadium (ABOVE) is home to the Vancouver Canadians. Sports lovers who'd rather avoid the crowds and the bright lights can spend an afternoon golfing in picturesque Stanley Park (PAGES 116 AND 117).

PAGES 116 AND 117: DAVID NUNUK / FIRST LIGHT PHOTOGRAPHY

WHILE THE PROFESSIONALS HAVE state-of-the-art facilities, athletes of all ages and abilities have access to the hundreds of sports fields that dot the city, including Livingston Park (LEFT), located near General Motors Place; a West Side park (TOP RIGHT); and Brockton Oval in Stanley Park, where the Rowing Club takes on UBC Old Boys Rugby Club (BOTTOM RIGHT).

WHEN NOT SKIING THE WINTER months away or sailing in the summer, Vancouverites can be found cheering in the stands at the city's sporting arenas. The crowd goes wild at General Motors Place, the Vancouver Canucks' new home (TOP). Canuck Pavel Bure (BOTTOM) and the B.C. Lions play a home game at B.C. Place Stadium (OPPOSITE, BOTTOM).

HENRY WOLF OF THE VANCOUVER Police Department's mounted squad lets his horse, Cambie, do the walking (BOTTOM RIGHT). Other officers aren't so lucky. These two constables (BOTTOM LEFT) are on foot patrol and have to pay for their mounts, which may not sound like such a bad idea to youngsters with a few coins in their pockets.

Patrick Reid (OPPOSITE), one of Canada's true diplomats, is highly regarded for his work as Commissioner General for Expo '86, Consul General in San Francisco in 1987, and Chair for Airshow Canada in 1989. Reid's 1995 autobiography is titled *The Wild Colonial Boy: A Memoir*.

▼ ROB KRUYT

WHILE MODERN-DAY ATHLETES compete during the Dragon Boat Festival (TOP), Bill Reid's *Spirit of the Haida Gwaii*, a $3 million jade canoe, depicts more traditional rowers and is a major tourist attraction at the Vancouver International Airport (BOTTOM).

THE ART OF LIVING WELL

THE MARINE LIFE AROUND
Vancouver is of inexhaustible
interest to the scientists and re-
searchers at the University of
British Columbia. The full splen-
dor of an Alabaster Nudibranch
can be viewed in the waters of
English Bay.

WHILE BRIDGES ARE NATURAL extensions of roads in Vancouver, ferries are critical for travel between the mainland, Vancouver Island, the Gulf Islands, and the Sunshine Coast.

FERRIES ARE MORE THAN JUST transportation—they are part of the unique culture and identity of the city and its environs. Drive your car on board. Park it. Forget it. Then lose yourself in a "cruise" through some of the most beautiful and untouched scenery the world has to offer.

PAGES 142 AND 143: DARWIN WIGGETT / FIRST LIGHT PHOTOGRAPHY

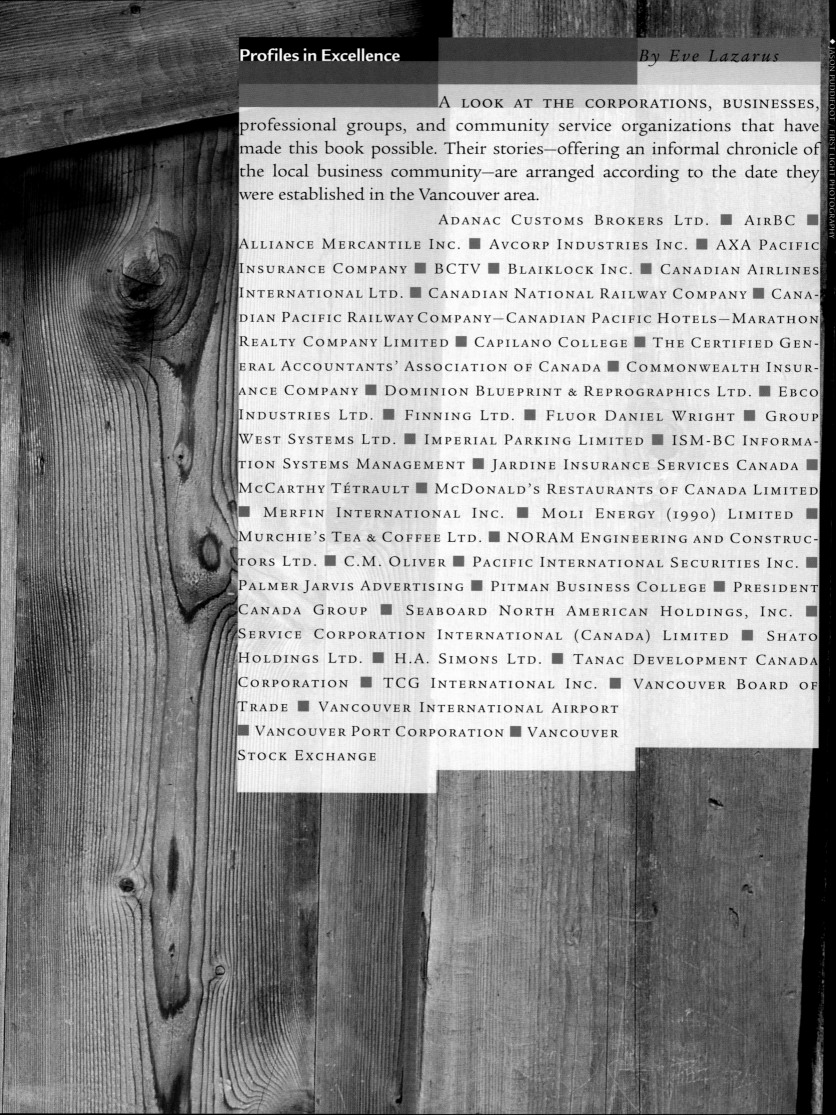

A LOOK AT THE CORPORATIONS, BUSINESSES, professional groups, and community service organizations that have made this book possible. Their stories—offering an informal chronicle of the local business community—are arranged according to the date they were established in the Vancouver area.

ADANAC CUSTOMS BROKERS LTD. ■ AIRBC ■ ALLIANCE MERCANTILE INC. ■ AVCORP INDUSTRIES INC. ■ AXA PACIFIC INSURANCE COMPANY ■ BCTV ■ BLAIKLOCK INC. ■ CANADIAN AIRLINES INTERNATIONAL LTD. ■ CANADIAN NATIONAL RAILWAY COMPANY ■ CANADIAN PACIFIC RAILWAY COMPANY—CANADIAN PACIFIC HOTELS—MARATHON REALTY COMPANY LIMITED ■ CAPILANO COLLEGE ■ THE CERTIFIED GENERAL ACCOUNTANTS' ASSOCIATION OF CANADA ■ COMMONWEALTH INSURANCE COMPANY ■ DOMINION BLUEPRINT & REPROGRAPHICS LTD. ■ EBCO INDUSTRIES LTD. ■ FINNING LTD. ■ FLUOR DANIEL WRIGHT ■ GROUP WEST SYSTEMS LTD. ■ IMPERIAL PARKING LIMITED ■ ISM-BC INFORMATION SYSTEMS MANAGEMENT ■ JARDINE INSURANCE SERVICES CANADA ■ MCCARTHY TÉTRAULT ■ MCDONALD'S RESTAURANTS OF CANADA LIMITED ■ MERFIN INTERNATIONAL INC. ■ MOLI ENERGY (1990) LIMITED ■ MURCHIE'S TEA & COFFEE LTD. ■ NORAM ENGINEERING AND CONSTRUCTORS LTD. ■ C.M. OLIVER ■ PACIFIC INTERNATIONAL SECURITIES INC. ■ PALMER JARVIS ADVERTISING ■ PITMAN BUSINESS COLLEGE ■ PRESIDENT CANADA GROUP ■ SEABOARD NORTH AMERICAN HOLDINGS, INC. ■ SERVICE CORPORATION INTERNATIONAL (CANADA) LIMITED ■ SHATO HOLDINGS LTD. ■ H.A. SIMONS LTD. ■ TANAC DEVELOPMENT CANADA CORPORATION ■ TCG INTERNATIONAL INC. ■ VANCOUVER BOARD OF TRADE ■ VANCOUVER INTERNATIONAL AIRPORT ■ VANCOUVER PORT CORPORATION ■ VANCOUVER STOCK EXCHANGE

1881	CANADIAN PACIFIC RAILWAY COMPANY—
	CANADIAN PACIFIC HOTELS—
	MARATHON REALTY COMPANY LIMITED
1887	VANCOUVER BOARD OF TRADE
1894	MURCHIE'S TEA & COFFEE LTD.
1898	PITMAN BUSINESS COLLEGE
1900	JARDINE INSURANCE SERVICES CANADA
1907	C.M. OLIVER
1907	VANCOUVER STOCK EXCHANGE
1912	DOMINION BLUEPRINT & REPROGRAPHICS LTD.
1915	CANADIAN NATIONAL RAILWAY COMPANY
1925	CANADIAN AIRLINES INTERNATIONAL LTD.
1933	FINNING LTD.
1936	ADANAC CUSTOMS BROKERS LTD.
1944	H.A. SIMONS LTD.
1946	TCG INTERNATIONAL INC.
1953	SEABOARD NORTH AMERICAN HOLDINGS, INC.
1956	EBCO INDUSTRIES LTD.
1959	ALLIANCE MERCANTILE INC.
1960	BCTV
1960	MCCARTHY TÉTRAULT
1962	IMPERIAL PARKING LIMITED
1965	COMMONWEALTH INSURANCE COMPANY
1967	MCDONALD'S RESTAURANTS OF CANADA LIMITED

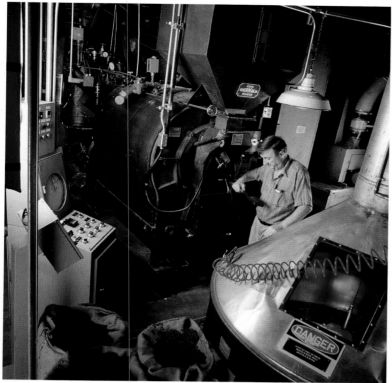

was to give Murchie's a facelift. Products have been repackaged and redesigned, and new lines have been added. More than 100 spices are now sold in attractive Mason-style jars. Gwen has also launched a focaccia bread spice and other trendy spice blends.

Murchie's has 12 retail locations in British Columbia that include tea and coffee bars, a 110-seat beverage bar in Victoria, and an outlet in the Memorial Library in West Vancouver. In February 1996 Murchie's moved its head office to Richmond and added a food and beverage take-out service. In addition, the company plans to open a 45-seat restaurant in the near future. In recent years Murchie's has also added a wholesale beverage division in order to service office coffee and restaurants, and has built up a wholesale grocery division as well as a healthy mail-order business, which boasts more than 25,000 customers—some as far away as Japan.

With an eye always on quality control, Murchie's operates two production kitchens that create many of Gwen Murchie's own recipes. Murchie has remained the company's chief taster, and she continues to focus a good deal of her time on developing new products. She put together the tea blend for the 1995 World Tea Party, while the Sutton Place Hotel and the Empress Hotel in Victoria both feature her blends at high tea every afternoon.

Murchie now sells a scone mix from a recipe handed down by her Scottish grandmother. Other new products include an Earl Grey Tea jelly; a Yuletide brew mix of spices for Christmas; iced teas that include mango, black currant, and orange flavors; and a creamy hot chocolate that appeals to children and adults alike.

Murchie uses the words "staff" and "family" interchangeably, and credits the loyalty and dedication of her employees for the company's success. She also believes strongly in community participation, and she has written a contract stipulating that store managers must be involved in the community.

Gwen Murchie has now been in the tea and coffee business for more than 30 years and is one of the city's top tea connoisseurs. She purchases teas and coffees from all over the world on the commodities market and imports them to Vancouver, where she creates all the company's recipes. She compares herself to a wine taster. "I got into the business without even realizing I was becoming a taster," Murchie explains. "I'm an information gatherer. I learned from Uncle Jim and I was fascinated by his love of the product, so of course I had to try it myself. In order to sell it, I had to know all about the product."

Coffee beans are roasted at Murchie's plant in Richmond (top left).

Gwen Murchie, President and owner of Murchie's Tea & Coffee Ltd. (top right)

Murchie's new head office is located in Richmond (below).

WHEN MARIE TOMKO BOUGHT PITMAN BUSI ness College, she inherited a dilapidated building, outdated instruction, and fewer than 40 students. Pitman—a household word in British Columbia for nearly a century—was teetering on the verge of extinction. ■ Founded in 1898 by the Richards family, Pitman had remained a family business

until Tomko purchased it in 1991 from the great-grandson of the original founders. Tomko saw the potential, and in 1993, a mere two years later, she received a regional award in the turnaround category from the Canadian Woman Entrepreneur of the Year Awards.

As the new president and CEO, she dusted off the cobwebs, moved the college to a downtown campus, updated the curriculum, and added the latest in technology. Now the name Pitman is not only synonymous with reliability and longevity, it is also on the leading edge in business training.

A School for the Future

A sense of history can still be felt in the college's new downtown location. Known as Birks Place, the renovated heritage building at the corner of Granville and Hastings streets is a stately edifice of marble and stone columns. But inside the college's 12,000-square-foot space, an investment of more than $500,000 in equipment and renovations has transformed the third floor into a state-of-the-art training facility. Thanks to the extra space, additional staff, and an emphasis on computer instruction for business administration programs, enrollment has grown by 60 percent. The college boasts a 100-station computer network from Novell, and Pitman is designated by Microsoft Canada as a Microsoft Solution Provider End User Training Centre.

Pitman trains students in the skills that are in high demand by employers, such as computer accounting, business computer applications, business administration/management, legal secretary, medical secretary, receptionist/secretary, and administrative assistant. The college now attracts highly qualified instructors. Although the minimum qualification is the provincial instructor's diploma, many faculty members have master's degrees and vast experience in business.

Computer lab instructors help students one-to-one (top right).

Marie Tomko, President and CEO of Pitman Business College (below right)

In the advanced computer application lab, students focus on training for the new economy with advanced computer applications (below left).

says the goal of the company is to develop a leading national investment and financial planning services company, which will be achieved through corporate acquisitions, the opening of new branch locations, and the recruitment of highly qualified professionals.

The investment and financial planning industry has entered an extremely high-growth phase that will extend beyond the 1990s into the next century as Canadians become increasingly concerned about retirement security and investment risks. Due to this phenomenon, known as the "graying of North America," experts predict that customers will continue to seek greater portfolio diversification and demand a higher level of knowledge and expertise from their financial advisers.

C.M. Oliver Capital Corporation

One of the C.M. Oliver Group's corporate finance arms is managed by a group of professionals with experience in investment banking, accounting, and securities law.

C.M. Oliver Capital's professionals work with both privately and publicly listed companies in structuring and managing equity and debt financing. "The opportunities that we seek are normally high-growth investment situations," says O'Brian. "We are looking for the enter-

prises and entrepreneurs that are creating Canada's new wealth over the next 20 years."

Public company financing includes emerging technology-driven enterprises in such areas as biotechnology, proprietary automated fabrication technology, wireless communications, and selected issuers in the natural-resource sector. "Canadian companies are well managed and have some of the best technology available. In addition, Canadian natural-resource companies are going out and exploring and developing on a worldwide basis," O'Brian says. "We are financing companies that need $5 million to $30 million, a niche that we are good at. We are selectively looking at emerging and small- to mid-cap companies."

"Our Edge"

People and ideas are our edge. This is why we will become one of Canada's top financial services organizations. Already this year, we have identified a number of high-growth situations in the technology and resource markets that have resulted in extraordinary returns for our clients," O'Brian says.

The C.M. Oliver Group of Companies is set to become a dominant player in the investment industry. The combined efforts of its operating subsidiaries allow the firm to cover all facets of investing and financing. C.M. Oliver's mission is to become one of Canada's premier financial services organizations by providing professional advice to clients on a domestic and international level.

Clockwise from top:
With close to 90 years in the business, C.M. Oliver understands that, although products and services are constantly changing, one thing remains the same: providing the best possible service for clients.

C.M. Oliver's executive management team—(from left) Keith Guelpa, George Hartmann, Daryl J. Yea, and William Sacre—is committed to building a premier financial services company both nationally and internationally.

P.J. Lovick knows that in order to succeed, one has to remain focused. While Lovick concentrates on creating successful commercial designs across Canada, he trusts his portfolio to the professionals at C.M. Oliver & Company.

THE VANCOUVER STOCK EXCHANGE (VSE), THE world's leading venture capital market, has played a vital role in building the economy of British Columbia and is now the source of finance for emerging businesses from North America, Asia, South America, Europe, Africa, and Australia. ■ Since its founding in 1907, the Exchange has

supported mineral exploration that led to important discoveries, such as the Hemlo gold mines and Voisey's Bay. Today, while continuing to raise capital for mining, the VSE provides venture capital for such diverse fields as high technology, manufacturing, biotechnology, and financial services.

The exchange focuses on companies needing investment to bring ideas and opportunities to life. Each year more than $1 billion (Cdn.) is raised for new ventures represented by the more than 1,500 companies listed on the Exchange. The VSE's slogan very simply summarizes its primary role: Where Business Starts.

In the words of President and CEO Michael Johnson: "We are committed to serving emerging businesses around the world as a key source of venture capital. Our regulations, trading

According to Michael Johnson, President and CEO of the VSE, "We are committed to service and our strategic positioning as the world's leading venture capital market." (top)

Native totem poles in Vancouver's Stanley Park provide a link between the city's beginnings as a small trading outpost and the dynamic international business centre it is today (bottom).

system, and the support provided to companies listed on the Exchange are geared to helping small and medium-sized companies that are ready to grow."

Help for Emerging Businesses

The majority of businesses listed on the VSE are junior or venture companies—smaller firms with promise. The Exchange's most appealing benefit is its willingness to help these young companies at a much earlier stage than other stock exchanges.

With minimal bureaucracy, the VSE works with businesses that need capital for research, development, exploration, or manufacturing, and provides support at a time when business loans and other traditional methods of financing may be hard to secure. The VSE understands the risk associated with new ventures—recognizing that with risk come new ideas and businesses that may grow into industry leaders.

Reaching into the Asia Pacific

As a financial centre on the Pacific, the VSE is placing growing emphasis on business opportunities in the Asia Pacific market. A special section of the Exchange is dedicated to companies based in China, Singapore, Malaysia, Hong Kong, Australia, and other centres of strong business activity. In bringing promising invest-

◄ JAMES O'MARA

ment opportunities from these countries to North America, the VSE is becoming an increasingly important link between the financial markets in the East and West.

Responding to global trends in business, the VSE is reaching out to international companies and investors. Almost 50 percent of all investment on the VSE comes from outside of Canada, primarily from the United States, Europe, and Asia. As this trend continues, the volume of venture capital raised will expand to support new listings, leading the Exchange toward a $2 billion year for new financing in the not-too-distant future.

Fair and Well Regulated

The VSE is carefully regulated to create a fair market for investors and listed companies. Among the first exchanges in the world to implement a computerized trading system and remove the traditional trading floor, the VSE is able to monitor market activity in an unprecedented

manner. Combined with a determination to protect investors, the VSE is operating with ever greater fairness.

While enforcing the rules and regulations necessary to be a well run market, the VSE works hard to provide efficient service to companies wanting to list on the Exchange.

Committed to Service

The VSE considers itself in the service business. It provides a wide range of information to assist investors and member companies. The staff

are trained to lead companies efficiently through the listing process with a great deal of support. The Exchange has committed itself to being second to none in its industry in terms of responsiveness to companies in search of venture capital.

As Johnson states, "The VSE will continue to grow and outperform the competition because we are committed to service, and we have given ourselves a very clear focus—we are the world's venture capital market."

Clockwise from top left:
Each year more than $1 billion (Cdn.) is raised on the Vancouver Stock Exchange to finance new ventures in mining, technology, manufacturing, oil and gas, and many other industries.

The VSE is the fourth most active stock exchange in North America and was the first exchange to implement a fully computerized trading system and eliminate the traditional trading floor.

With its position on the Pacific Rim, the VSE services investors and listed companies from Canada, the United States, Latin America, and the Asia Pacific, playing a key role in Vancouver's development as a major international financial centre.

▶ JAMES O'MARA

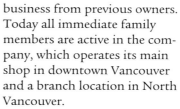

THE ROOTS OF DOMINION BLUEPRINT & REPRO-graphics Ltd. are firmly planted in the history of Vancouver. For more than 85 years, the firm has served the city's architects, engineers, and construction contractors, and has evolved alongside many of Vancouver's most famous historical buildings. ■ Although Dominion Blue primarily duplicates and

From top:
Dominion's full drymounting and laminating facilities add the finishing touch to a Megachrome™ digital colour print.

A Dominion sales representative explains to a customer the different digital printing services available at Dominion Blue.

John Bingham Sr., President of Dominion Blue

enhances the work of architects, engineers, and contractors, a wide variety of other businesses—including graphic designers, advertising agencies, retail customers, and legal firms—also rely on the company for high-quality document reproductions, expert advice, and fast turnarounds.

"We know the demands of the industry," says President John Bingham Sr. "Our skilled people use the latest state-of-the-art technology to ensure that all reproduction work clearly and accurately represents the original document. Our turnaround time is measured in minutes and hours, not days or weeks. We have to remain highly motivated at all times. Our customers appreciate our one-stop approach to solving their reprographic needs with cost-effective solutions to meet their critical deadlines."

Originally founded in Vancouver in 1912, Dominion Blue became a family business in 1985 when Bingham, who has successfully managed the company since 1977, was given the opportunity to purchase the

business from previous owners. Today all immediate family members are active in the company, which operates its main shop in downtown Vancouver and a branch location in North Vancouver.

Bingham coined the term THE REPROFESSIONALS® to describe Dominion's quality of business. "We do reprographics professionally," he says. Dominion has followed a long tradition of using only the latest equipment and newest technology once it becomes available, ensuring the highest quality reproduction possible to its customers. However, traditional reprographic services—blackline and blueline prints, oversize 36-inch photocopies, and specification printing—remain key components of the company's business day.

As the reprographics industry has continued towards digital innovation, Dominion Blue has kept pace by utilizing such technology as the DocuTech™ Electronic Publisher, a digital printer that produces print jobs directly from electronic files and/or hard copy originals. "Our customers can now print what they want when they need it, eliminating costly document storage and wastage," says Bingham. "Documents can be digitally stored and updated when required, keeping valuable originals current at all times for future reprints."

Dominion's digital imaging department provides CAD services utilizing the Indigo Plotter/Printer that reproduces digital drawings at record speeds—about 600 prints (36-by-48-inch) per hour—providing customers with

fast turnaround and top-quality reproductions of their design work. Another first for Dominion was the introduction of Vancouver's graphic design community to Megachrome™ large-format, digital colour prints produced directly from computer files. Dominion also provides digital colour laser copies as well. All digital originals can be sent via modem to the company's Open Express™ 24-hour Bulletin Board System. Dominion's full drymounting and laminating facilities add the finishing touch to all customers' reproduction work whether it's big or small, colour or black-and-white.

Dominion Blue also has the only black-and-white photographic department available in downtown Vancouver for high-quality archival reproductions such as photo prints and mylars, PMTs, negatives, and clear film positives for screen printing. The firm also specializes in restoring old architectural and engineering drawings.

Since the early days of the 20th century, Dominion Blue has witnessed ongoing technological change in the reprographics industry. As the first Canadian to be President of the International Reprographics Association and as an active participant in numerous trade associations—such as Northwest Reprographics Association, ReproCAD, and The Vancouver Board of Trade—Bingham intends to keep his company first in the minds of commerce and industry professionals through continued research of technological changes to ensure that its customers' expectations are always reached or exceeded.

company opened three facilities in Poland. The latest acquisition in 1993 was the Caterpillar dealership in Chile that operates as Gildemeister S.A.C. and has seven branches, three depots, and parts and repair services at six mine sites.

In Canada Finning has full sales, parts, and service facilities throughout British Columbia, as well as Alberta, the Yukon, and part of the Northwest Territories. There are 28 full sales, parts, and service facilities plus eight service depots and 23 resident service representatives.

Focus on the Customer

A framed certificate hanging on the wall in Finning's reception area is a printed reminder to employees of the first and most important point of the company's mission statement: "to meet and exceed the expectations of each customer." Next to it is a framed business statement summing up the company's philosophy: "Our business is to consistently provide the best solutions to people who move, harvest, and transform goods or materials so they can meet the needs of their customers."

Finning never forgets its customer. "We differentiate ourselves from our competition in our ability to focus attention on specific customer needs," says Shepard. "We can do this because we have the resources to provide focused services and can invest in the training of our people. We strive for individualized attention based on an intimate understanding of each customer's situation."

This understanding and ability to serve the niche markets led to the introduction of small machines like the backhoe loader that could be used by a sole owner or small business. In the 1980s Finning opened four rental centres in Prince George, Langley, Calgary, and Edmonton, and now offers a full line of rental products including midsize excavators and wheel loaders for the construction industry. Finning recognized that rentals provide a safety valve for

contractors, enabling them to meet production goals without a large capital outlay.

Finning fully believes that a customer is also a partner, and to prove the point, has entered into a number of strategic alliances with its customers. In some cases the company has put a full-service shop on a customer's site. Finning's knowledgeable and committed employees meet with customers often on a monthly basis to review any problems they may be experiencing.

"If we can look after our customers' equipment needs, then they can focus on what they do best. They can get on with the business of selling their products to their customers," Shepard says.

Caring for Others

A nother goal etched on the wall in Finning's Vancouver office says "We care about the well-being of each other." Finning means its employees, of

course, but it doesn't stop there; the company is committed to the community.

In 1995 employees donated $170,000 to the United Way and the company matched with an equal amount. An employee incentive program encourages volunteer work with Finning matching donations dollar for dollar. The Power Tour is another success. World-class amateur wrestlers visit schools in British Columbia and Alberta to demonstrate wrestling holds and deliver a message to youths on the dangers of substance abuse. Since the sponsorship began six years ago, the Power Tour has delivered its message to more than 160,000 students. Finning is also a well-known contributor to health, education, youth programs, the environment, arts, and sciences.

By caring about its community, its employees, and its customers, Finning Ltd. has met the many challenges addressed by its mission statement.

A Cat 312 excavator places shot rock into a retaining wall in this West Coast subdivision development (top).

Working at 6,000 feet above sea level, this Reedrill SK-45i drills 40-foot holes in preparation for blasting at this limestone quarry in the Rocky Mountains (bottom).

As Adanac Customs Brokers prepares to meet the challenges of the next century, the British Columbia-based company remains focused on two things: providing unparalleled customer service and building on the fact that the company has been employee owned and operated since its inception in 1936. ■ Adanac is the largest

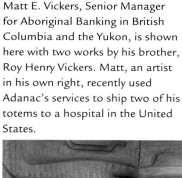

Matt E. Vickers, Senior Manager for Aboriginal Banking in British Columbia and the Yukon, is shown here with two works by his brother, Roy Henry Vickers. Matt, an artist in his own right, recently used Adanac's services to ship two of his totems to a hospital in the United States.

customs brokerage firm located at Vancouver International Airport, but the company proudly remains a medium-sized firm with clients ranging from one-person operations to international conglomerates. Company President Barton Ramsay says that it would be difficult for a larger company to compete with Adanac's personalized customer service, which is offered to every client without exception.

"It's a full-service concept," says Ramsay. "We will 'custom clear' the goods when they get to Canada, arrange for local delivery, or send it to our warehouse. If the job requires distribution to multiple destinations, we'll do that as well. We offer the services of a local agent when remote services are required, and we can also monitor the shipment and make sure all the deadlines are met."

Ramsay also notes that customs brokerage requires a specialized knowledge of international rules and regulations, and while it is an integral part of Adanac's business, it is also only one facet of the company's broad range of services. "In the new economy—where inventories are generally smaller than in the past—customers often need goods 'just in time,'" says Ramsay. "Clients not only require customs clearance, they also want their goods cleared with speed and accuracy."

A Wide Range of Services

Throughout the past 60 years, Adanac has adapted to changes in the industry. Since its inception, the company has evolved from specializing entirely in customs brokerage to offering an entire range of import/export services. Through Adanac International Forwarders Ltd., the company handles all aspects of international freight forwarding, logistics, break-bulk consolidation, warehousing, and trade show and exhibition shipping.

Large engineering firms frequently use Adanac for complicated turnkey operations. For instance, machinery that is imported from different points around the globe must first arrive in Vancouver and then be shipped throughout Canada,

usually when time is of the essence.

Adanac is also one of the few project forwarders in Vancouver with the ability to ship large exports anywhere in the world. The company recently shipped an entire acid manufacturing plant—which was fabricated in British Columbia—to China. Adanac made all arrangements related to shipment of the plant, including transporting the facility by barge to North Vancouver, loading the ship, and ensuring the plant's safe arrival in China several weeks later.

Adanac's experienced staff makes complicated logistics planning appear effortless. Employees have complete information regarding each client's products and particular handling requirements, and all are trained in the intricacies of each mode of transportation, whether it be air, sea, road, or rail. For example, if the firm is handling a shipment of machinery, an Adanac employee selects the right ship for the goods, organizes the transportation to the ship (as well as the loading and unloading), designates an agent to sail with the cargo, and supplies marine insurance for all contingencies involved.

Personalized Customer Service

Adanac owns and operates two 11,000-square-foot warehouses in close proximity to the company's airport location. The two facilities provide clients with an alternative to public warehousing and enable the company to offer a complete range of services. For example, Adanac can handle all the details involved in Canadian distribution for small manufacturing or import companies that do not have the volume or revenues to warrant opening an office in Vancouver. "It enables people to start up a business with no outlay until they reach a point where they can open an operation on their own," says Adanac's Managing Director, Ross Davidson. "We know the goods, we know the product, and we know the client."

A Global Network of Offices

Through a partnership with United Shipping Associates, Adanac is electronically linked with brokers and freight forwarders in more than 400 strategic locations in 60 countries around the world. This networking system allows the company to have local control of cargo 24 hours per day, regardless of where suppliers or customers are located. Adanac's staff can instantaneously track cargo, provide verification of shipment, or log into an airline's network in order to confirm a shipment's arrival.

Because Adanac is the exclusive agent for Medallion Shipping Lines and Medallion Air Cargo, the company can offer competitive sea and air rates as well as competitive group rates on cargo insurance and marine bonds. In addition, world travellers may rely on Adanac's international network of offices, which allows clients to make large or expensive purchases in other countries and have the company's experts arrange the packing, travel, and clearance documents for the shipment's safe arrival.

Adanac's services are not exclusively dedicated to the international transfer of goods. The company's knowledge of shipping and wide range of contacts across Canada have enabled it to provide huge savings for domestic customers wishing to ship goods from coast to coast.

Ramsay and Davidson note that Adanac has made a strategic decision to remain small on the customs brokerage side of the business, while expanding in the areas of freight forwarding and warehousing in order to offer customers optimum service. "The size of the customs brokerage business is restricted by the quality of service that it gives," adds Ramsay. "And that's what we want to continue to do. We will offer personalized service to clients with unusual needs."

Weekly meetings are held in the head office boardroom to discuss new business and plans for the future (above).

Adanac Warehouse Division operates as a staging area for worldwide exports (left).

Adanac's head office is located at the Vancouver International Airport (below).

H. A. Simons Ltd.

THE PROFESSIONALS AT H.A. SIMONS LTD. understand that to stand still in today's competitive marketplace often means to slide backwards as competitors advance. For this reason, the company has grown from a small Vancouver-based operation to become one of Canada's largest engineering firms with a work force of more than 2,500

Counterclockwise from top left: A Simons employee discusses Nexgen machine start-up with a vendor's representative.

MacMillan Bloedel's Port Alberni No. 5 paper machine Nexgen Conversion Project, earned Simons the 1996 Consulting Engineers of BC Award of Merit. With the new paper machine, this client became the only producer of lightweight coated paper on the West Coast of North America.

H.A. Simons' project for Howe Sound Pulp and Paper Ltd.—located in Port Mellon, British Columbia— earned the 1992 Schreyer Award— the highest award for Canadian Consulting Engineers.

employees worldwide. The company also maintains full-service offices in Australia, Chile, Indonesia, New Zealand, and the United States.

In 1944 the company's founder, Howard Simons, saw great potential for British Columbia in the emerging bleached kraft pulp industry, which supplies producers of high-grade paper products such as letterhead and stationery. More than half a century later, Howard Simons' son, Tom, heads a company that specializes in providing complete engineering services for resource industries such as forestry, mining and metals, and energy, in addition to pulp and paper manufacturing. Through other offices and partnerships around the world, the company has diversified its offerings in order to serve a wide range of industries, including specialty chemicals, food and beverage, ports and terminals, manufacturing, film and fibre, and infrastructure.

Simons has evolved from a company that once functioned strictly as an engineering consulting firm into one that actually designs and manages

engineering projects for its clients. "A few years back, we were a very traditional consulting engineering company that functioned as a resource for the client," says Brian Bentz, Simons' President and COO. "We have gone beyond that now. We are moving into areas where we are providing services and providing them in ways different from what we traditionally did as a consulting engineer."

Known throughout the world as an innovator in project design and management, Simons offers a complete range of basic engineering services as well as specialized disciplines, such as architecture and environmental engineering, in order to address its clients' needs.

Economic and design modelling tools—such as PASCE (a 3-D plant design and modelling system) and Simons IDEAS™ (a dynamic simulation

tool)—allow the client to test designs and concepts before making costly capital investment decisions. "We can offer a range of services from project concepts to pre-feasibility studies, feasibility studies, definition engineering, construction management, commissioning, start-up assistance, and training," says Bentz. "We really focus on working closely with the client in order to identify which of our services make the most sense for each project."

The Simons Mission

Simons' vision is to be a global business that is committed to meeting the expectations of its customers for successful solutions, systems, and facilities. The company's focus is on the excellence of its people, its use of technology, and partnering with others. In order to accomplish this

from a huge machine to a tiny high-precision instrument. We have the facilities to complete all design phases of a manufacturing operation, including fabrication, welding, machining, assembly, and testing."

Ebco has been a pioneer in adapting technological advances to the needs of the modern marketplace. Over the 40 years since its founding, the company's manufacturing capabilities have expanded from metal dies into heavy machining and fabrication, precision machining, aircraft tooling, and cyclotron technology, among a host of other products and services. Helmut Eppich describes Ebco's work as experimental. "We do a lot of prototype manufacturing where we have a real advantage over other companies," he says.

By 1993 Ebco's manufacturing diversity expanded considerably to include many divisions and spinoff companies. Through the company's divisions—the Heavy Machining, Heavy Metal Fabrication, Light Metal Fabrication, and Tool and Die divisions of Ebco Industries Ltd.; Epic Data International Inc.; Ebco Technologies Inc.; and Ebco Aerospace—a broad range of specialized products and components are developed and marketed for an expanding worldwide customer base.

Ebco Industries Ltd.

Today Ebco Industries Ltd. is one of the largest custom manufacturing facilities in Western Canada. The Heavy Machining division serves the forestry, pulp and paper, mining, power generation, petrochemical, nuclear, aerospace, and defence industries. Its products include heavy machinery for primary industries, such as grinders, crushers, pulp dryers, mining shovels, steam and gas turbine housings, and underground tunnel-boring machines.

In the Heavy Metal Fabrication division, many different projects are in manufacture at various stages of completion. Examples of recent projects

undertaken by this division include the manufacture of large hydraulic mining shovels for India; complex tooling for the assembly of the U.S. Air Force C-17A military cargo plane; and kilns and mill shells for various primary industries, as well as maintaining a busy program of mining equipment, both new and repair.

At the Light Metal Fabrication division, recent projects include aircraft tooling and mobile and stationary radar antenna arrays for the U.S. defence program. The division also manufactures steel products for the forest, health, hydroelectric, and retail industries.

Items include sealed conveyor systems, laundry and linen carts, street lamp standards, and shopping bag dispenser machines.

The Tool and Die division employs highly skilled die makers who design and manufacture dies both for in-house use in the company's Stamping Department and also on contract to other customers, as well as diversified and complex components for the aerospace/defence industry and for medical prostheses.

Epic Data International Inc.

An example of the Ebco Group's resourcefulness

Clockwise from top:
A job well done. Some of Ebco's employees pose in front of a Mobile Miner cutter head used for tunnel boring, which was manufactured for the Robbins Company of Kent, Washington.

Epic Data International Inc. is the world's leading supplier of fully integrated, high-performance data collection systems. Epic's employees—shown in front of the head office in Richmond, B.C.—service more than 750 customers worldwide.

The Light Metal Fabrication division of Ebco is known for its work in the aerospace and defence industries. Shown is an antenna array structure for a mobile ground-based radar system.

This 22-foot diameter autoclave locking ring for the aircraft industry was formed from seven-inch-thick steel, welded in sections, and machined at Ebco's Heavy Machine shop.

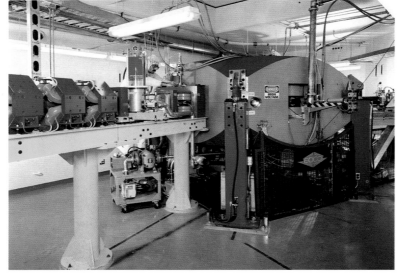

Ebco's TR-30 radio-isotope production cyclotrons are the most advanced and efficient in the world, a reflection of the technological excellence of Ebco Technologies Inc.

This long, critical aircraft structural component was machined by Ebco Aerospace on a five-axis CNC gantry profiler. The machining line is the largest of its kind in Canada.

can be seen in the process that led to the creation of Epic Data International Inc., a subsidiary that creates fully integrated electronic data collection systems. In 1965 Helmut Eppich began searching for a computer system that would track the company's growing number of jobs, employees, inventory, tools, and machines. The search revealed that there was no such product on the market, and leading computer systems manufacturers could offer no cost-effective solutions. Undeterred, Helmut Eppich decided to invent and build his own system, which is still in use at Ebco today. In 1974 Epic Data was incorporated as a new division, offering its first data collection system to the general public that same year.

The new company developed specialized systems for the University of British Columbia Library, the Montreal Post Office, and the Mexican Soccer Lottery, among others, in addition to its line of data-recording devices designed for tracking manufacturing activities and inventories. Epic Data has become a world leader in this niche market of high-performance, fully integrated data collection systems, and its products are widely used by many Fortune 500 companies around the globe. Companies such as Boeing, Lockheed, General Electric, and Air Canada use Epic Data systems.

Ebco Technologies Inc.

In the early 1970s Ebco Industries Ltd. built key components of the 500 Mev cyclotron at TRIUMF—the TRI Universities of Meson Facility—which is Canada's subatomic particle research facility located at the University of British Columbia. "We were the first ones and the only ones in Vancouver to bid on the project," says Helmut Eppich. "Our competitors were all afraid—they could not see how they could carry out this high-precision high-quality work. I was not worried about it. I was used to changing and adding capabilities as demanded by the marketplace."

Building on a unique partnership with TRIUMF, Ebco Technologies Inc. was established to commercialize the expertise of the world's most experienced design team in cyclotron and nuclear chemistry technology. Ebco Technologies Inc. has now produced five commercial and medical cyclotron systems, which are widely acknowledged to be the best in the world.

Ebco Aerospace

In 1987 growing potential business from industry giants—such as Boeing, McDonnell Douglas, and Raytheon—prompted the creation of Ebco Aerospace Inc., a state-of-the-art CNC precision machining facility that is the largest of its kind in Canada. A wide variety of commercial aircraft components are manufactured, including landing gear components, flap hinge control mechanisms, fuselage frames, spar webs, and components for Boeing's new 777 aircraft.

Ebco Aerospace has also manufactured booster rocket rings for space shuttles and major structural components for the Mobile Base Servicing System for the International Space Station, which is being jointly developed by NASA, Canada, Japan, nine members of the European Space Agency, and Russia for completion by 2002.

The centrepieces of Ebco Aerospace's state-of-the-art precision machining facilities in Delta are four CNC three-spindle five-axis gantries mounted on a 14-by-190-foot bed. "We are specializing in large parts because our machines have one of the largest capacities in North America for this type of equipment," says Helmut Eppich. The plant's computer-based control facility makes Ebco Aerospace an obvious choice for major aircraft manufacturers.

Corporate Values

Ebco's corporate values are enshrined in a corporate culture that spans all divisions. As the company grew, Helmut Eppich and Ebco's board members adopted a list of codes that became the foundation of the company. These codes stress three main principles: the value of the person, the value of perfection, and the value of prosperity—in that order. This value system was honored in 1990 when Ebco received *B.C. Business* magazine's Entrepreneur of the Year award. According to Helmut Eppich, "Modern corporations that want to compete in the global market must have a universal value system."

Ebco values, recognizes, and celebrates diversity among its own work force. According to the company's code, the value of the person has three primary aspects: love, dignity, and respect. Under these three categories, there are 30 subvalues, such as respect for the individual's

ethnic, cultural, and religious backgrounds. Ebco's nurturing of such values has been rewarded in the form of the first ever issued Race Relations Award from the government of Canada, a Workplace Awareness Award from the Canadian Mental Health Association, and recently, a Cultural Diversity Award from Surrey-Delta Immigrant Services Society. In addi-

tion, a tribute to diversity among the company's employees can be found in the collage of 48 national flags on display in the lobby of Ebco's corporate offices in Richmond.

Four decades after its founding, Ebco is truly a worldwide corporate and industrial leader. By relying on the multiple skills and diversity of its work force, all divisions of Ebco will continue to prosper well into the future, bringing a new generation of expertly crafted products to the world's marketplace.

Clockwise from top:
A collage of flags from 48 nations hangs in the front lobby of Ebco Industries Ltd. The collage celebrates the unique multicultural and multiskill diversity of Ebco's 500 employees.

Ebco's manufacturing diversity also includes small items such as these moth cages used in the orchards of the Okanagan in British Columbia.

Scientists, engineers, technicians, and other highly skilled workers from Ebco Technologies Inc. surround a positron-emission tomography (PET) cyclotron they had just completed for Seoul National University in South Korea .

Major structural components for the International Space Station were machined by Ebco Aerospace. The 23 subassemblies machined by Ebco will be used on the Canadian Mobile Base Servicing System.

Alliance Mercantile Inc.

SINCE ITS FOUNDING MORE THAN 36 YEARS AGO, Alliance Mercantile Inc. has evolved from a small import trading company into a national marketing/distribution firm that has developed unique business associations with some of the world's leading manufacturers. ■ A marketer of a diversified range of consumer products—including rubber

gloves, industrial and recreational rainwear, rawhide dog bones, lint rollers and brushes, textiles, and rubber safety footwear—Alliance is the Canadian leader in sales for most of these categories. An important key to the company's success has been the business partnerships it has developed with such multinational companies as Australia-based Pacific Dunlop's Ansell division, the world's largest manufacturer of latex products; Helmac USA, the world's largest manufacturer of lint rollers and lint brushes; and Malaysia-based Golden Hope's Viking Askim, a global leader in the manufacture of high-tech rubber safety footwear.

The Early Days

Alliance Mercantile Inc. has been through several changes over the years—in name, location, and focus. Originally located in a 2,000-square-foot warehouse in Gastown, the company began as Alliance (Western) Sales Ltd. in 1959, a local import trading company specializing in general merchandise. When the company moved to the edge of Yaletown in 1975, the name was changed to Alliance International Sales Ltd. to reflect its expansion across Canada and through the western United States. Within five years, the company expanded again with the purchase of 1178 Hamilton Street in Yaletown, a 54,000-square-foot, six-floor, turn-of-the-century warehouse.

In 1982 the company made its final change in name to Alliance Mercantile Inc. and significantly altered its marketing focus. "It became obvious that if we didn't specialize and become pseudomanufacturers in some areas, we would be just one of a zillion other importers," says Joel Sardone, founder and CEO of Alliance. The company began to shed its trading lines, moving out of the general merchandise business and focusing on higher-velocity consumer

wares such as rubber gloves, soft goods, and rawhide. "Today we are no longer just importers. We are marketing, packaging, manufacturing, and distributing people," says Sardone.

The company focused its attention on becoming expert in specific product categories, designing and developing programs unique for the Canadian market. Kaz Nakamoto, Vice-President of Finance and one of Alliance's founding employees, emphasizes the contributions the company's staff has made in the evolution of the company. "At each turn," he says, "we were fortunate enough to have people from varying backgrounds lead us through the changes and add new dimension to the company."

Looking Out for the Customer

In the early 1980s, when a recession forced consumers to become more value conscious, Alliance saw an opportunity in developing a no-frills product line of consumable wares that could meet this need. In 1981 Alliance Mercantile Inc. launched one of the first comprehensive generic-branded programs in Canada under the

Alliance is one of Canada's leading suppliers of rubber footwear, specializing in logging and chain saw boots (near right).

Ansell is the world's largest manufacturer of latex products (far right).

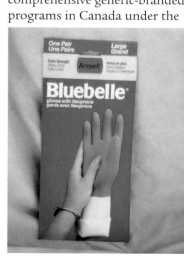

also responded to client needs by developing practices in emerging specialties relating to aboriginals, technology, the environment, entertainment, and liaison with governments.

A Winning Record

McCarthy Tétrault is one of the leading litigation firms in Canada, having some of the nation's most renowned counsel. Over the years, the firm has contributed many partners to the Canadian judiciary, including the Supreme Court of Canada.

The firm represents clients in every aspect of litigation before all levels of the federal and provincial courts as well as before regulatory and administrative tribunals. It handles cases dealing with every kind of dispute, and its litigation group includes lawyers with expertise in a large number of specialized fields of advocacy.

The firm has acted and is currently acting in some of Canada's most significant public inquiries and lawsuits. Of course, not all cases find their way into the headlines. The firm's barristers bring many matters to a successful conclusion outside the courtroom. McCarthy Tétrault recognizes that clients wish disputes to be resolved not only successfully, but economically and with a minimum of disturbance to their affairs. Alternate dispute resolution is today an important means by which the firm assists its clients in achieving their goals.

When It's Personal

McCarthy Tétrault also assists and advises clients in respect of their personal legal affairs. In resolving a personal crisis, planning for retirement, making plans for a future generation, buying or selling a home, or seeking advice on all matters relating to immigration, clients can be confident that their lawyer at McCarthy Tétrault will serve them with understanding, courtesy, expertise, and personal care.

▶ DOMINIC SCHAEFER

The firm has been rendering services of the highest quality to its clients for more than 140 years.

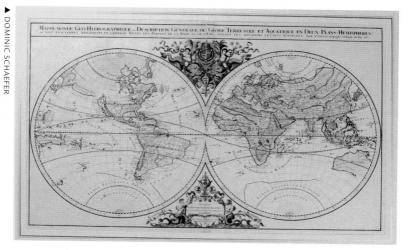

▶ DOMINIC SCHAEFER

World-class legal skill, detailed knowledge of Canada's successful institutions and regulatory models, and competitive pricing give McCarthy Tétrault an edge in advising governments and businesses internationally.

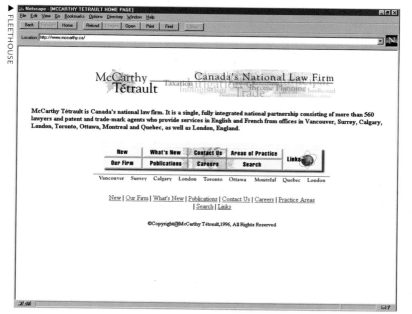

▶ FLEETHOUSE

The firm's resources allow it to provide clients with an extra margin of service—quick response and cost efficiency—using the right tools and the specialized knowledge, varied talents, and experience of its lawyers.

IMPERIAL PARKING LIMITED (IMPARK) WAS founded more than three decades ago. The company's rapid ascent to become Canada's largest parking management company and a major player on the international stage is the result of a carefully crafted plan engineered by Impark Chairman, President, and Chief Executive Officer Paul Clough.

Clockwise from right: Imperial Parking attendants greet customers as they arrive.

B.C. Place is one of Imperial Parking's numerous locations throughout North America. During B.C. Lions football games, it is not unusual for this lot to be filled to capacity.

Impark's parking equipment ranges from simple ticket-dispensing machines to sophisticated, fully automated computer-based operating systems that can take cash, credit, or debit cards. Its System IV parking machines are now used everywhere from parking lots to campgrounds and marinas.

Since his start with the company in 1969, Clough has seen the parking industry grow from a simple one-person operation with a cigar box to hold cash to a very sophisticated, competitive, and high-tech industry requiring large financial resources and years of experience.

When Impark completed an initial public offering in 1994, it was already a national company, operating across Canada and the United States. The capital injection allowed Impark to further expand eastward and to successfully compete in the lucrative and fast-growing Asian market. With the acquisition of Citipark in 1995—Impark's biggest competitor—the company doubled in size, expanded into several more Canadian cities, and opened the door for more expansion south of the border.

Impark has now established branch offices in Taipei and Hong Kong. "Our expansion is aggressive, but at the same time, focused and cautious," Clough says. "We have resisted the temptation to expand much more until we are absolutely certain that these activities benefit the bottom line and that our standards of service are not compromised in any way."

The Business of Parking

Impark's story began back in 1962 when Arne Olsen, a MacMillan Bloedel sales representative, couldn't find a place to park his car. Olsen found a house that had been partially

destroyed by fire, persuaded the owner to knock it down, and charged his colleagues $5 a month to park on the site. When that lot filled up, Olsen found another. With partner John Adams, he opened 13 lots over the next four years, some of which included gas stations and car washes.

Parking cars may seem like a simple business, but it requires particular attention to detail. The core of the management business is carried out by the parent Impark and two subsidiaries: Robbins Parking Service and Imperial Parking, Inc., the U.S. division.

Impark has grown from humble beginnings into a full-service business that oversees more than 1,390 properties in 50 North American cities, and more than 3,000 employees. "We want to be as self-sufficient as possible," says Clough. "As a result, we build our own signs; manufacture a complete line of parking equipment; print our own tickets; handle all of our computer requirements; do all of our own research and development; build, design, and finance new parking structures; and even offer a comprehensive security service. As far as we know, we are the only parking company in North America that offers a complete turnkey operation."

In 1995 Impark created Compupark Systems and expanded its equipment marketing capacity. Impark's parking equipment ranges from simple ticket-dispensing machines to sophisticated, fully automated computer-based operating systems that can take cash, credit, or debit cards. Its System IV parking machines are now used everywhere from parking lots to campgrounds and marinas.

What sets Impark apart from the competition is leading-edge technology. The company spends more than $1 million every year on research and development. It was the first company to introduce high-tech security to the parking business and the first to introduce a parking concierge. The company developed the first self-park system that accepts credit card payment. It was also the first to accept debit cards and it developed a system enabling customers to add value to these cards through Visa and Mastercard. Impark's ability to create and adapt its technology won the company the contract to install the ticket vending machines for the West Coast Express, and at the same time, found a lucrative niche in a new market.

Sophisticated computer-based systems developed by Impark were put to use more than a decade ago to create City Collection Company—the parking enforcement side of the company. Using special hand-held computer monitoring equipment, City is able to track violations, issue notices, and ultimately collect fees and fines. Based initially on service to pri-

vate sector clients, City is now working with various cities and municipalities to provide cost-effective collection systems.

Customer Service Drives the Company

Realizing the value of its clientele, Impark holds customer appreciation days. "We try to recognize our customers during different times of the year. We give away such things as flowers, candy canes at Christmas, and cinnamon hearts on Valentine's Day," Clough says. "We have staff during the summer who do nothing but wash windshields. We do these little things that we think make a difference—things that people wouldn't expect a parking company to do."

Impark has come a long way since Arne Olsen operated the business from the trunk of his 1949 Chevy, but the company's philosophy has not changed. It is still a people business. "We decided early on that if we were going to stay in the parking business we had to improve the image," says Clough. "Our success is the result of committed staff who understand the importance of superior customer service."

Clockwise from top left: Parkades for Waterfront Centre, Canada Place, and Granville Square are managed by Imperial Parking.

A research and development staff member works on a System IV meter.

Company executives review plans for the company's Waterfront Centre parkade.

COMMONWEALTH INSURANCE COMPANY, A dynamic operation located in the heart of Vancouver, is better known within the insurance industry than it is to the general public. This is unfortunate because the company's origins make it one of Vancouver's more colorful companies, as well as one of the city's most successful. ■ When

the present management began its operations in 1965, it was a small company with only $10,000 in capital. Five years later, when John Watson—the company's Chairman, President, and CEO—joined the company, he had a difficult time drumming up business. Today, however, Commonwealth's capital exceeds $125 million, and the company has an A.M. Best rating and a Standard & Poor's rating of A for excellent, indicating superb financial soundness. Today Watson has little trouble attracting new clients to his company.

John Watson, Chairman, President, and Chief Executive Officer of Commonwealth Insurance Company

DAVID GRAY

For the past 20 years the company has held an annual reception that initially was attended by about 15 brokers. Last year, more than 600 friends and associates were present at what has become one of the main industry events in Canada.

Commonwealth is a major writer of all classes of commercial property, casualty, oil, gas, and petrochemical insurance to brokers throughout Canada, the United States, and abroad. In a country where the majority of the property and casualty insurance market is dominated by foreign companies, Commonwealth is 100 percent Canadian-owned and continues to expand its facilities worldwide.

"We've become more traditional as we have evolved, but we were anything but traditional in the early days," recalls Watson. "We were such a small company then. We had no status in the United States, and we weren't rated by any of the rating bureaus, so the only business that came our way involved the difficult risks that nobody else wanted. We would get high rates for the business, but the exposure was very high also."

While all insurance companies are in the business of risk, Commonwealth mainly deals with major risks. The average premium is around $100,000, and with 3,000 policies in place around the globe, the company now produces gross revenues approaching $300 million.

Commonwealth is licensed in all provinces of Canada to engage in all areas of insurance other than life insurance. In the United States, the company is also licensed in the state of Delaware and approved in 41 additional states. The firm

opened a second office in Seattle, Washington, in 1989 in order to facilitate the expansion of its growing business in the United States. In 1995 the Seattle operation became Commonwealth Insurance Company of America, a fullfledged subsidiary of the Vancouver company that is licensed to write business in Washington State.

In 1993 Commonwealth's parent company, Reandex International Limited, was absorbed by Fairfax Financial Holdings Limited, a financial services holding company with assets of $5.5 billion and an investment portfolio totalling more than $3.15 billion. The corporate reorganization made Commonwealth a wholly owned subsidiary of Fairfax. However, because of Fairfax's decentralized policy, Commonwealth continues to run autonomously.

Operations

Commonwealth has four areas of underwriting operation. About 50 percent of the business stems from the U.S. and Canadian Commercial Property divisions. These two divisions insure exposures throughout North America, and when natural disasters strike, they inevitably incur their proportion of resulting losses.

In the past several years the United States especially has been hit with a spate of major disasters, including Hurricane Hugo in 1989, Hurricane Andrew in 1992, and the Northridge earthquake in California in 1994. Fortunately for Commonwealth, the carefully engineered spread of risk and the utilization of the worldwide reinsurance facilities mitigated

When McDonald's Canada introduced pizza to its menu board in 1991, seven years of testing 145 types of pepperoni, 30 different sausages, and 75 cheese blends preceded the launch.

Changing the Face of Quick-Service Food Retailing

The first McDonald's in Canada was a small nondescript red-and-white-tile restaurant with no seating and three takeout windows. Hamburgers were sold at 18 cents each. The menu was limited to hamburgers, cheeseburgers, filets of fish, fries, shakes, soft drinks, and hot apple pies (the Big Mac came along in 1968). At the opening, the demand was not anticipated. On the first weekend, the operator ran out of meat and was handing out rain checks for free hamburgers to disappointed customers.

Today McDonald's serves more than 2 million customers across Canada every day and is one of the country's top 10 employers with more than 70,000 employees, nearly 25,000 of them in the West. The company's purchases also account for thousands of jobs in industries that supply it with food products and other supplies and services.

Have You Had Your Break Today?

McDonald's and its agency partners in marketing and advertising have helped to make the Golden Arches and Ronald McDonald the world's most recognized symbols. Its ultimate success, however, relies on the ability of its people to fulfill the consumer expectations generated by its marketing.

Dedication to quality, service, cleanliness, and value (QSC&V); community service; and quick response to consumer demand and changing tastes and lifestyles are all a part of keeping McDonald's at the forefront.

Marcoux says the momentum will continue through a grass-roots philosophy that is completely customer driven. The mission of every McDonald's employee is to satisfy 100 percent of the customers 100 percent of the time.

McDonald's constantly develops and changes systems, products, and marketing strategies to meet customer demand. When consumers asked for environmentally conscious initiatives, McDonald's began a waste reduction action plan to reduce, reuse, and recycle. It responds to changing tastes and lifestyles with such items as fresh salads and low-fat shakes, yogurt, and muffins as well as McDonald's Pizza and the Arch Deluxe, the "burger with the grown-up taste."

McDonald's is consistently number one in restaurant sales and Marcoux means to stay on top by expanding the number of restaurants and adding streamlined express outlets for customer convenience. "Retail has changed a lot since 1967," he says. "Huge malls are consolidating all their services in one location and we have to go where the people are and not expect them to come to us."

Entering 1996, McDonald's Canada had more than 50 express locations—mini-McDonald's in shopping malls, hospitals, Wal-Marts, and gas stations. Such locations are expected to grow by about 20 per year.

Community Commitment

Being a valued part of the community is important to the Golden Arches. Marcoux looks for franchisees and managers who will be a part of the community. "We want our people to be committed to giving something back to their communities."

Marcoux himself demonstrates this commitment by example. He's the Honorary Chair of Special Olympics in Western Canada, a Variety Club Golden Heart Award recipient, an avid booster of Ronald McDonald Houses in five Western Canadian locations, President of Giant Steps in Greater Vancouver, and a member or past member of hospital boards and other educational and social institutions. He also was the first to provide corporate backing to Rick Hansen for his Man-in-Motion round-the-world wheelchair odyssey. Says Marcoux, "We feel our commitment in each community is amply rewarded by the loyalty of our customers."

Clockwise from top left: Located in Burnaby, the Western Region Office of McDonald's Restaurants of Canada fosters an atmosphere where ideas can flow.

The first McDonald's in Canada was a small nondescript red-and-white-tile restaurant with no seating and three takeout windows.

Today McDonald's has numerous ultramodern restaurants—such as this one in Guildford—that feature large play areas for children.

For his Man-in-Motion round-the-world wheelchair odyssey, Rick Hansen received a cheque from McDonald's, presented by Marcoux.

FIFTY YEARS AGO, ARTHUR AND HERBERT Skidmore opened their first automotive glass shop in New Westminster, British Columbia. The brothers worked in the shop by day, and by night, they fitted plate glass windows into city buildings. The Skidmores invested all their earnings back into the business and acquired two more

Clockwise from top left:
Apple Auto Glass is a network of 124 franchise stores in Canada that specialize in automotive glass repair and replacement, as well as automotive upholstery.

In 1993 TCGI purchased Novus Inc., a franchise windshield repair operation. Novus has 900 franchises and 1,600 agent-operated locations.

Glentel is a growing wireless and personal communications company serving the needs of Canadians for satellite phones, cellular phones, paging products, two-way radio applications, and residential long-distance service.

TCGI is a mixture of corporate and franchise operations. In Canada all 165 Speedy Auto Glass locations are operated by the corporation.

retail automotive replacement glass stores in 1959.

Today, TCG International (TCGI) is a world leader in the repair and replacement of automotive glass. The senior Skidmores remain active on the board and oversee a corporation with more than 3,000 employees and more than 1,700 locations in North America and around the world. Hard work, a responsibility to employees, and a dedication to customers are the values that have guided the company throughout its history, helping

it to grow into an operation earning approximately $400 million per year.

TCGI is a mixture of corporate and franchise operations. In Canada, for example, all 165 Speedy Auto Glass locations are operated by the corporation, and Apple Auto Glass is a network of 124 franchise stores in Canada that specialize in automotive glass repair and replacement, as well as automotive upholstery. The company also owns 21 Autostock Distribution centres. In Quebec the company operates

320 corporate and franchise operations through its subsidiary Autostock Inc. In 1993 TCGI purchased Novus Inc.— a franchise windshield repair operation—and became the fourth-largest automotive franchise operation in the world. Novus has 900 franchises and 1,600 agent-operated locations.

TCGI recently diversified into manufacturing after acquiring a 30 percent interest in Rioglass, S.A.—an automotive glass plant in Spain. The plant will service the company's European customers as well as North American retail and distribution operations.

The company has an interest in the emerging field of wireless communications. In 1989 TCGI purchased Glenayre Electronics (now Glentel), and entered the business of retail sales and distribution of wireless communications products. It seemed a natural fit since Speedy Auto Glass locations throughout the region had been successful at selling cellular phones for Cantel.

Glentel is a growing wireless and personal communications company serving the needs of Canadians for satellite phones, cellular phones, paging products, two-way radio applications, and residential long-distance service.

The reasons for TCGI's success in the increasingly competitive industry of automotive glass products are obvious: superior customer service, an emphasis on quality products and workmanship, ongoing employee training, and a strong market share. While automotive glass products will remain an integral part of the business, TCGI predicts that wireless communications will play an increasingly important role in the future. The company has incorporated its retail and distribution experience in order to become a national "wireless one-stop retailer" and establish a leading position in this developing industry.

1968   CAPILANO COLLEGE

1968   SERVICE CORPORATION INTERNATIONAL (CANADA) LIMITED

1969   THE CERTIFIED GENERAL ACCOUNTANTS' ASSOCIATION OF CANADA

1969   PALMER JARVIS ADVERTISING

1969   SHATO HOLDINGS LTD.

1975   BLAIKLOCK INC.

1976   GROUP WEST SYSTEMS LTD.

1979   AXA PACIFIC INSURANCE COMPANY

1980   AIRBC

1981   PACIFIC INTERNATIONAL SECURITIES INC.

1982   NORAM ENGINEERING AND CONSTRUCTORS LTD.

1983   VANCOUVER PORT CORPORATION

1986   AVCORP INDUSTRIES INC.

1988   FLUOR DANIEL WRIGHT

1989   MERFIN INTERNATIONAL INC.

1989   PRESIDENT CANADA GROUP

1989   TANAC DEVELOPMENT CANADA CORPORATION

1990   MOLI ENERGY (1990) LIMITED

1991   ISM-BC INFORMATION SYSTEMS MANAGEMENT

1992   VANCOUVER INTERNATIONAL AIRPORT

THE MAIN CAMPUS OF CAPILANO COLLEGE IS nestled on a forested mountainside on the north shore of Burrard Inlet—an expanse of ocean away from downtown Vancouver, but only a 20-minute drive. Wooded trails weave through park-like surroundings, taking students from the newly completed library and classroom complex to the multimedia language resource centre, the performing arts theatre, and the Sportsplex.

The beauty of the campus and the quality of education attract students from all over the province, and increasingly, from around the world. Students come to Capilano for its innovative educational programs—a personalized setting that fosters learning—and to receive the skills and training needed for their chosen careers. Since Capilano first opened its doors in 1968, it has developed an enviable reputation as one of British Columbia's outstanding colleges. In addition to the main campus in North Vancouver, regional campuses in Squamish and Sechelt serve the communities of Howe Sound and the Sunshine Coast.

With more than 6,000 students, it is one of the largest community colleges in the province. Capilano offers a complete range of academic, career, and vocational programs, and is noted for its strong university transfer academic program, which is the equivalent of the first two years of an undergraduate baccalaureate program.

Focused on Student Success

At Capilano students are the first priority. The college has earned a reputation for teaching excellence and innovation, and has distinguished itself by its commitment to student success. The quality of instruction and qualifications of faculty are extremely important to the college. All of the instructors are experts in their fields and Capilano is proud of the fact that all the faculty members are dedicated to teaching. Many of the faculty in the academic disciplines hold doctorates and maintain research associate status with one of British Columbia's two leading universities. The career and vocational faculty are active in their respective business and professional communities and maintain close ties to the business community.

Several years ago Capilano was the first college in the province to initiate follow-up studies of its graduates. "This was, and continues to be, the best way to ensure the college's responsiveness to student needs," says Capilano President Dr. Greg Lee. "In surveys of recent graduates 98 percent stated that their education at the college was worthwhile, and more than 80 percent of graduates ranked the quality of teaching they received as good to excellent. We feel this feedback is the most important we receive. It is our goal to ensure that our students come first—not only at the college, but in all of their pursuits."

Staying on the forefront of leading-edge technology is also critical to the success of the college. Through a local area computer network linked to other colleges and universities in British Columbia with access to the Internet, students can literally do their research anywhere in the world. The latest in videoconferencing technology links students at the Sechelt and Squamish campuses with those in North Vancouver, and gives them access to distance education courses offered through Capilano and the Open Learning Agency.

"The college is committed to developing new and innovative programs in response to market demand. For example the Applied Information Technology Program, in which students use sophisticated

From far left to right: CANASEAN Program graduates pose with the Honourable Raymond Chan, Secretary of State Asia-Pacific, and former Capilano College President Douglas K. Jardine at the program's closing ceremony. Program Director Edwin Wong is pictured on the left.

Capilano College President Dr. Greg Lee

The Library plaza is at the heart of the North Vancouver Campus.

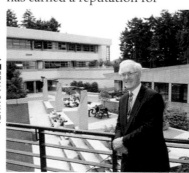

▲▼EDNA SAKATA

echnology and work closely with industry, is the only one of ts kind in Canada," Lee says. "Programs like these give students the practical skills and knowledge they need to achieve their occupational goals."

An International Outlook

Capilano is strongly committed to international education and plays an active role in the development of programs, many of which are unique to Canada. Says Lee, "We are involved in international education because we believe that our programs will prepare students to succeed in further studies and to achieve occupational goals and personal aspirations. We provide high-quality academic experiences and relevant activities, and welcome international students as a vital part of our college."

Sometimes the success of a particular program surprises even the college. The CANASEAN Program began in 1989 as a seminar and workshop series where Canadian and Asian businesspeople could meet, share ideas, and gain an understanding of each other's business culture and customs. Those who have attended the program speak about the personal relationships that have formed and the insight gained from being on the job with business entrepreneurs, managers, and executives of different industries. The pro-

gram quickly became a regular feature of Capilano's international programs, and is offered for approximately four months every fall.

The Asia Pacific Management Cooperative Program is another of Canada's most innovative postgraduate business programs. This unique two-year diploma program is designed to help Canadians access opportunities in the Asia Pacific region in a practical and effective way, offering students a year of highly focused study in combination with a year of paid work experience in Asia. "The program contributes substantially to the development of an international business community in Canada," Lee says. "Our graduates have gone on to challenging managing positions, both in Canada and in Asia."

Currently more than 70 employers work with the college on a regular basis. They include B.C. Gas International, Canadian Airlines International, the Economist Intelligence Unit, the Royal Bank of Canada, Price Waterhouse, and Enterprise Thailand Canada.

Capilano has led or been involved in a number of international development projects in Thailand, the Philippines, Vietnam, Malaysia, and China.

Forging business links is a vital role of Capilano College—for its own future growth and for the growth of its students and the surrounding community. A leader in both education and the community, Capilano College has secured its place in Vancouver.

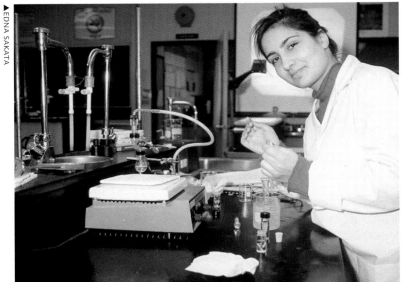

▲ EDNA SAKATA

Clockwise from top:
Capilano College is noted for its strong university transfer academic program, which is the equivalent of the first two years of an undergraduate baccalaureate program.

Staying on the forefront of leading-edge technology is critical to the success of the college.

The main campus in North Vancouver has evolved with the construction of several impressive new facilities, while maintaining one-third of the 34-acre campus for second-growth forest preservation.

▲▼ EDNA SAKATA

FROM ITS BURNABY OFFICE, SERVICE CORPORA-tion International (Canada) Limited (SCI Canada) is changing the face of its industry. Now the second-largest provider of funeral and cemetery services to Canadians, SCI Canada is bringing innovative management practices and a strong customer empathy to the industry. ■ SCI Canada grows by acquiring quality funeral homes and cemeteries across Canada. The company has more than tripled its number of locations in the past six years and now owns in excess of 100 locations consisting of funeral homes, cemeteries, and crematoriums in British Columbia, Alberta, Quebec, and Ontario.

Humble Beginnings

When Robert L. Waltrip took over his family funeral home in Texas, he had no idea that 34 years later his company would become the largest funeral service enterprise in the world with revenues of more than $1.6 billion a year. Waltrip's involvement began in 1962. He bought a second funeral home in Houston and then a third. He invented the "cluster concept," and found that he could substantially reduce costs and improve service by sharing the staff, the limousines and hearses, and the preparation facilities of all three centres. The clustering concept is central to the success of the company and is employed in every city in which Service Corporation International (SCI), the parent company, operates.

In 1969 Waltrip took SCI public, and the previous year began his advent into Canada. Waltrip bought funeral homes in Winnipeg and then established the company in Vancouver with the purchase of Forest Lawn Funeral Home and Memorial Park, Ocean View Burial Park, and Mount Pleasant Funeral Home.

A Growth Industry

President Jack Gordon says the company's expansion activities are directed toward satisfying a large future market for its services. "The death rate is going to increase dramatically over the next 25 years," he says. "The baby boomers are now starting to make more funeral arrangements as their parents age, and they will soon be getting to the age when they will be looking at prearranging their own funerals."

The "graying of North America" is behind SCI's aggressive expansion. More people over age 65 are alive than at any other time in history. As well, high start-up costs are discouraging new competition, and many small family-run businesses are finding that continuing to manage the business without the financial headaches involved is exceedingly attractive.

Gordon looks at the demographics of a city before deciding to acquire or build a funeral home. He targets funeral homes in cities with large populations older than age 65. In the Lower Mainland, SCI Canada owns six funeral homes and two cemeteries, including a recently constructed facility in Surrey to cater to that city's growing population. Other properties, such as the Ocean View Burial Park and Forest Lawn Memorial Park in Burnaby as well as First Memorial Funeral Services of North Vancouver, are being

From far left to right:
The Abbey Mausoleum is one of the outstanding features of Ocean View Burial Park in Burnaby.

Forest Grove Columbarium is in a setting of natural beauty at First Memorial Funeral Services in North Vancouver.

SCI established its presence in Vancouver with the purchase of several properties, including Forest Lawn Funeral Home and Memorial Park in Burnaby.

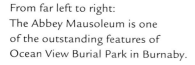

requirements. The company gets every shipment from point A to point Z, advises on methods of distribution, and, where possible, consolidates goods to save its clients money.

Blaiklock continually searches out the most advanced technology available. The company's extensive electronic data interchange (EDI) network includes monitoring the movement of goods, facilitating remote tracing, and providing statistical reports and billing summaries. An increasingly important function is the receipt of invoices electronically from clients or their suppliers. These documents are used to print the Canadian customs invoice for customs clearance in advance of the shipment arriving at the border. The invoice information is also automatically used to prepare the customs declaration that is electronically transmitted to customs authorities. Transaction processing times have been dramatically reduced from days to a few hours using this process.

The Government Affairs Group

Although the North American Free Trade Agreement (NAFTA) was designed to free up the barriers to trade, the fact is that companies in the import/export field need the consulting services of experts in the customs brokerage business now more than ever before.

Blaiklock has recognized that need and created its Government Affairs consulting group with the best credentials in the industry. Through personal contact and seminars, the Blaiklock Government Affairs group helps keep Blaiklock clients informed of the changing role of government and how it affects their business.

The Partnership Approach to Business

Blaiklock employees invest a significant amount of time listening to the changing business needs of their clients and finding new services to further

Blaiklock Inc. handles all kinds of products moving all over the world. Here, a new container crane arrives for the Port of Vancouver (above).

Even alpacas, headed for Hagensborg, British Columbia, need the help of a customs broker and freight forwarder to ensure proper transportation and to handle the reams of paperwork (left).

facilitate the movement of their goods and thus improve their profitability.

"A few years ago we asked ourselves, 'Where do we want to be in the year 2000? Do we want to be the biggest?' And we said, 'Not necessarily, but we certainly want to be the best,' " Robinson says. "We try to form true partnerships with our clients by providing them with the most up-to-date information and making sure that all the things that are necessary for customs are in place." Voluntary compliance with customs ensures the company a good government profile, and goods are typically cleared faster and without problems.

Since 1876 the changes in transportation and growth of information and technology have been staggering. Since the time when nine employees handled the Blaiklock business using paddleboat, steam and sailing ships, rail, and wagon, the values of the company have endured. The Blaiklock name is still synonymous with leadership, progress, and a total commitment to customer service. William Musgrave Blaiklock would be proud of the company he initiated more than 120 years ago.

"Here in the 1990s we can only guess at the changes in technology, transportation, and geography we'll see by the end of our second century of service," says Robinson. "We do know, whatever the challenges, we'll still be leading in our field to help keep our clients leading in theirs."

IN THE HIGH-TECH BUSINESS, WHERE CHANGE IS the only constant, Group West Systems Ltd. has managed not only to survive, but to flourish. Its customers, a virtual shopping list of industries, include British Columbian institutions like the Keg Restaurants, B.C. Hydro, Clearly Canadian, and Rogers Sugar. ■ Group West was established by a group of hardware, software, and industry specialists in 1976. Since then it has helped more than 500 companies with information needs. These customers range from first-time users to very large and sophisticated operations, and the variety of industries and years of experience mean that Group West's ability to match business needs with technology systems is unparalleled in the industry.

When the company first opened its doors two decades ago, the personal computer was still a thing of the future. "Can you imagine a system now that doesn't have PCs? It's a dramatic difference," says company President Bill Ste. Marie. "It was all batch processing systems when we started. You would feed cards and tape into the computer and reports would come out the other end."

In those days the company focused on business systems that coincided with the release of IBM's System 34. As technology evolved and advanced, Group West grew with it. Today the company focuses on strategic planning—where information systems support business requirements.

"Usually there are two things that a company wants to do—increase their sales and reduce their costs. We will help them come up with the business strategies to do that," Ste. Marie says. "People are doing things the way they did them 10 years ago because they worked 10 years ago, but they may not work today. Now people are looking at technology as a strategic advantage. What we try to do is focus on what's going to give our customers a competitive advantage, what's going to make them the low-cost provider, what's going to increase their market share."

Changing with New Technology

Group West has a staff of more than 60 employees, with 80 percent working in the technical support area. It shows the company's unwavering commitment to service and support and the reason why it is the recognized leader in helping clients take advantage of the latest advances in information systems technology such as radio frequency, imaging, electronic commerce, client/server applications, and the Internet.

The company has developed a method for rapid application development in a client-server environment, and new products include the Windows NT Server and the Internet. "The Internet is the hottest thing to hit information technology since the introduction of the PC," says Ste. Marie. "There is a whole group of products and services surrounding the Internet. Companies can expand their markets at a very low cost by distributing products and services through Internet-enabled applications. There are a lot of applications that lend themselves very well to implementation over the Internet."

While Group West offers a full range of products from predeveloped application software to custom-tailored solutions, the company's strength is its ability to marry the best possible technology with a specific business need.

Group West executives discuss the potential impact of the Internet on their clients (left).

Group West is a leader at developing client/server applications that work (right).

"Every business is different in what is strategic for them, and that's where our consulting comes in. Our clients are the only people who really understand their business, but we know a lot more about technology and we can help the customers open their minds to other possibilities," says Ste. Marie.

A company wanting to improve its marketing position may find software that supports telemarketing, direct marketing, or perhaps a database for its sales staff—improving efficiency and, ultimately, the bottom line. Customers are demanding electronic commerce where they can order 24 hours a day, seven days a week, and where goods arrive on time, every time. Group West can also help a company looking to reduce costs by re-engineering its business and implementing systems to support new processes such as warehouse automation, radio frequency, or bar coding. "We will come up with a whole information technology strategy to support their business strategy," Ste. Marie says.

Unlike other companies that develop their own software and attempt to solve every problem with the same solution, Group West researches everything on the market. That way, says Ste. Marie, the company is in a position to understand what all these products are capable of doing and then to provide customers with the best solution. "The approach that we've taken is to understand what the prob-

lem is, then match the right technology to that problem. If we don't already know about it, we will go out and look into it," he says. "We spend a lot of time and effort just researching products so we can make sure our customers get the benefit of that knowledge."

Toward the Future

While keeping pace with emerging technologies, Group West has also grown and expanded over the years. In 1992 the company opened an office in Winnipeg, and shortly afterward, another office was established in Calgary. In the past three years, smaller branch offices have been set up in Saskatoon, Seattle, and Los Angeles with plans to further expand into the U.S market.

Ste. Marie believes more employees will work from home-based offices as the companies

of the future cut the high overheads of office space, and travel time becomes prohibitive. "We can dial into any one of our customers' computers from anywhere in the world," he says. "There is very little that we can't do for our customers."

Clockwise from top: According to Bill Ste. Marie, President of Group West Systems Ltd., "Our goal is to focus on what is going to give our customers a competitive advantage."

Group West can help a company reduce its costs by implementing technologies such as radio frequency and bar coding.

Group West's marketing team reviews a new product that will help clients prepare for the year 2000.

Group West is proud of its "wall of fame." Ray Medway, Vice-President of Marketing, puts up another satisfied customer letter on the wall.

THE KEY WORD IN AXA PACIFIC INSURANCE Company's name is "Pacific." Unlike many of Canada's other major insurance companies, which are tending more and more to an Eastern-based centralized structure, AXA Pacific is firmly rooted in the West. When asked to comment on the company's rather unique regional approach,

President and Chief Operating Officer Bob Vickerstaff says, "The success of this company rests in the fact that it has been built from the ground up using Western creativity and innovation. We have built a large general insurance company by doing things just a little bit differently than they do back East. What we are striving to be is the 'biggest little' insurance company in the West." AXA Pacific presently has offices in Victoria, Kelowna, Prince George, Edmonton, Calgary, and Winnipeg, in addition to its headquarters in Vancouver.

Vickerstaff's recipe for success may appear to be a simple one, but it has proved to be effective in improving the company's bottom line. In 1995 gross written premiums of slightly more than $145 million made AXA Pacific the largest property/casualty insurer in British Columbia and a major force on the Western Canadian insurance front.

Although the company has undergone a number of name changes throughout its corporate lifetime, the constant has always been its Pacific orientation and its commitment to serving the insurance needs of those who live and work in the West. What began as Paragon Insurance Company in 1979 became Laurentian Pacific in 1983. Ten years later change came again when the company was sold and renamed Boreal Pacific. In November 1995 the company was acquired by the French-based AXA Group of Companies and renamed AXA Pacific Insurance Company. AXA Group is the 10th-largest insurance group in the world, represented in 23 countries on four continents, and has Canadian writings in excess of $1 billion.

Philosophy of a People Company

More than most other industries, insurance is a people business and AXA Pacific's unwritten creed of building by attraction rather than promotion is the foundation upon which the company has grown. By attracting and hiring the best people, AXA Pacific has assembled some of the industry's top professionals who, in turn, through their superior knowledge and service, attract new business, fuelling the engine of fiscal growth. AXA Pacific's team of professional,

From left to right:
Bob Vickerstaff, AXA Pacific's President and Chief Operating Officer, attributes much of the company's success to a simple recipe, one of attraction rather than promotion.

With its head office in picturesque Vancouver, AXA Pacific brings a truly Western Canadian perspective to the insurance marketplace.

From left to right:
True to its Western Canadian roots, AXA Pacific has tailored its products to meet the needs of industries indigenous to the West, such as forestry.

AXA Pacific Insurance is a proud member of the worldwide AXA Group of Companies, represented in 23 countries on four continents.

Offering unique products to the construction industry, it has been said that AXA Pacific is insuring the West from the ground up.

dedicated employees is the number one reason that the company has continued to succeed year after year.

Based on this philosophy, the staff of just five in 1979 has grown to become a close-knit team of 200 employees working out of seven branches. Employees are recruited in each region for their experience and knowledge of the trading area and then empowered with the autonomy to make local decisions. In this way the company is able to bring a localized understanding to each region it serves in the marketplace.

In addition to this regional approach and commitment to hire top people, the company's strategy also calls for the delivery of the best products and services in the industry. This is a strategy that has allowed AXA Pacific to avoid competing solely on the basis of price in favor of being a quality company that competes through better delivery of services. It's a philosophy so ingrained that the company has registered and proudly displays its trademark: Quality Insurance Pays™.

Products

Unlike direct-writing insurance companies, AXA Pacific distributes its products through a network of independent insurance brokers who deal directly with the customer. In this manner, each customer receives personal attention and customized products designed to meet his or her particular needs rather than being subjected to a generic prepackaged approach. Representing AXA Pacific throughout the West are 450 professional independent brokers.

True to its Western Canadian roots, the company has tailored and customized its products to meet the needs of those industries indigenous to the West, such as forestry, oil and gas, and construction. On the construction side, for example, not only does the company offer contractors the broadest property and liability products available but also combines a full-service surety facility. Surety underwriting, or bonding as it is also known, provides the financial guarantees that afford the security for a thriving construction industry and a healthy economy. With surety writings of slightly more than $15 million in 1995, AXA Pacific is the largest surety writer in Western Canada and the third largest in the nation.

Along with such traditional lines as automobile and habitational, AXA Pacific also specializes in all types of commercial, marine, boiler and machinery, long-haul trucking, and professional liability insurance. As Vickerstaff points out, "A good part of the success of this company is directly attributable to our broad product line, as some of the classes which are written are anticyclical in nature. In a cyclical business such as insurance, a loss in one area can easily be offset by a profit in another. For AXA Pacific, this has meant years of steady profits."

Future

The insurance industry is expected to face numerous challenges in the years ahead. Technology, changing consumer buying habits, and the need for more efficient delivery of products will alter the roles insurers and brokers currently play. The challenges will be great, yet the same Western ingenuity and creativity that got AXA Pacific to where it is today will see it through the changing times ahead. Of course the primary objective—the delivery of quality insurance products tailored to the needs of the West—will remain the same. The only difference will be the need to be a little smarter and a little better.

From its location on the Pacific Rim and as a fully integrated member of the worldwide AXA Group, AXA Pacific Insurance is remarkably well positioned to support its network of independent brokers and the customers they serve. The dynamics of change present a whole new range of opportunities for the insurance industry and the future certainly looks bright for the "biggest little" insurer in the West.

PAINTED ON THE WALL IN AIRBC'S HANGAR AT the Vancouver International Airport is a message with letters two feet high. Visible to all of AirBC's employees and customers, it reads: "To be the best regional airline in the world renowned for: Customer Service Superiority, Safety, Technical Excellence, Employee Pride, and Profitability." It is

the first indication of how seriously senior management takes the company's mandate. Wholly owned by Air Canada, the regional airline operates within Western Canada from Victoria to Winnipeg, as well as trans-border flights such as Vancouver-Seattle, Vancouver-Portland, and Calgary-Spokane. AirBC links communities in the West to Canada's major city centres and to the rest of the world through Air Canada.

Al Graham, president of AirBC, explains the airline's current philosophy: "Air Canada and AirBC have decided that we are going to be the best in the West. We have the lion's share of the market everywhere except in Western Canada. The potential is clearly here, and we're going after it."

AirBC began in 1980 when the Jim Pattison Group purchased and amalgamated six small coastal airlines. Three years later, it purchased its first Dash-7 aircraft and became a feeder airline for Canadian Pacific Airlines. In 1987 AirBC was sold to Air Canada and became a regional partner in the airline's network. In 1996 AirBC sold off its float plane division and completely moved into a new era. The move cut costs, improved efficiency, and allowed the airline to focus on a fleet of Dash-8 aircraft, state-of-the-art turboprops, and British Aerospace 146 jets. With more than 300 flights per day to more than 28 destinations, AirBC is now the thirdlargest airline in Canada and the largest regional carrier in the country.

Focus on Customer Service

Formerly the vice-president of customer service for Air Canada, Graham believes customer service is the single most important focus for the airline. "We are a regional carrier, and we have to deal with the realities of our environment," he says. "We can't dazzle customers with caviar and champagne. Seventy percent of our flights are basically under one hour, so we have to be very good at the basics, which is getting people from A to B on time, in a comfortable environment, with friendly caring people."

Employee pride is the driving force behind customer service at AirBC. The airline has implemented service quality training and recognition programs for all 1,000 employees.

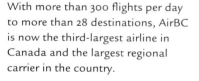

With more than 300 flights per day to more than 28 destinations, AirBC is now the third-largest airline in Canada and the largest regional carrier in the country.

Freshly painted aircraft, new interiors, a new business class section, improved on-time performance, and new company facilities are all part of Graham's goal to instill employee pride and to be the best in the West.

AirBC was the first regional airline in the West to initiate a dedicated business class on its jet service. Business travellers can now reserve their flight through the Executive Class reservations line as well. There is separate check-in and priority baggage delivery. In the air, the business traveller has a larger seat, more leg room, and a selection of magazines and newspapers. On longer flights, passengers enjoy a meal service with a selection of French and Canadian wines.

AirBC has doubled its flights between Victoria and Calgary, and increased its service between Vancouver and Edmonton, as well as between Vancouver and Calgary. This expansion of services offers the airline's customers a more convenient schedule and better access to the Air Canada network.

A market niche for AirBC is its growing Cargo Division.

"We want to be the same-day specialists," says Graham. AirBC already generates significant cargo revenue and is among the top producers for regional airlines, and Graham sees this as a huge opportunity for the future.

Nothing Short of Technical Excellence

With a 98 percent dispatch reliability, AirBC has one of the best reliability records in North America. Graham vows this figure will soon increase to 99 percent. Anything less is just not good enough, he says. Along with the company's excellent on-time performance record,

AirBC is also renowned for its safety and maintenance record, and Graham is adamant about keeping it that way.

Aircraft appearance and cabin cleanliness are of equal importance. A shabby-looking airline causes customers to lack confidence as people today want to travel in a clean and comfortable environment.

Of the five goals in AirBC's mission statement, profitability is more a result than a goal. Graham says that if the airline is renowned for its customer service, technical excellence, safety, and employee pride, then profitability will be the result.

AirBC's state-of-the-art fleet includes DeHavilland Dash 8-100 aircraft (top) and British Aerospace 146 jets (bottom).

Pacific International Securities Inc.

SINCE COMMENCING OPERATIONS IN 1981,
Pacific International Securities Inc. (PI)—an employee-owned investment dealer—has endured two lengthy recessions, as well as the stock market crash of 1987, and has seen the banks move from providing traditional financial services to taking over many of the country's established securities

firms. Yet, by offering clients a superior level of service and sound financial management, the company has made a profit every year, and gained a reputation for integrity, excellent investment performance, and outstanding growth.

An Investment Philosophy

From the start, the company's founders knew they could not compete with the country's major financial institutions and that the company's long-term success would come from choosing a market niche. While still offering a full spectrum of investment products and services, they began to specialize in the venture capital market. With years of experience in Swiss and Canadian banking, business ownership, and management, PI CEO Max Meier and Executive Vice-President John Eymann offered clients an investment philosophy that promoted stability with the opportunity for above-average growth. "Brokerages are traditionally up and down. We try to be more stable, to be more like a Swiss bank," says Meier.

Hands-on involvement is important to Meier and

Eymann, who expect their investment advisers and analysts to always put the customer first. The addition of Senior Vice-President Lawrence McQuid in 1985 brought yet another dimension to PI's growth. McQuid's strong administrative and management skills ensure that the firm provides the highest level of service to its clients. Employing more than 130 people, PI now serves in excess of 30,000 public, private, corporate, and institutional clients throughout the world.

A Full-Service Investment House

Being a full-service investment dealer, PI offers a comprehensive range of products including equities, bonds and debentures, mutual funds, registered retirement savings plans (RRSPs), registered retirement investment funds (RRIFs), and options and derivatives. As a member of the Vancouver, Alberta, and Toronto stock exchanges, the firm participates in a variety of financings. This provides its clients with opportunities to invest in emerging growth companies at an early stage of their development

where PI feels the best potential for gains are available.

PI is one of the most active brokerage firms trading on the Vancouver Stock Exchange (VSE)—an international venture capital market specializing in financing and trading small and medium-sized companies. These companies come from a variety of different industries, ranging from resource-based companies to high-technology firms. Whatever the industry, nearly all the companies are in the early stages of growth; they often have no track record, and they have difficulty raising money through traditional means for mineral exploration, research and development, or expansion. While the risk is higher, these new businesses can offer enormous returns to investors.

For example, in 1995 PI was one of the first brokerage firms to recommend Bre-X Minerals Ltd. to its clients. This Canadian resource company was exploring for gold in Indonesia, and was trading its stock for $0.45 per share (post split) at that time. Those who took PI's advice sold the stock months later for a substantial profit.

A Focus on Research

Finding top-performing emerging companies such as Bre-X reflects PI's strong emphasis on research. Headed by Vice-President Bert Quattrociocchi, PI maintains one of the largest research departments in Western Canada. Its analysts are constantly searching for well-managed small- and mid-cap companies with dominance in their respective fields, and assessing whether there are catalysts for change to boost the stock prices for these

PI's Executive Committee includes (from left) Marty Reynolds, Bert Quattrociocchi, Max Meier, Bob Blades, John Eymann, and Larry McQuid.

HPI/CAMERON HERYET

companies. Performance results have been outstanding and, as a result, PI's analysts are often quoted in local and national financial publications.

An International Perspective

PI was one of the first firms of its size to place such a heavy emphasis on research. It's not unusual—firsts are important to the company and its founders. It was one of the first to aggressively pursue international business, actively seeking banks and other institutional investors in Europe and Asia.

It saw the interest by Hong Kong companies to list their shares on the VSE, and it was the first investment dealer to sponsor the inter-listing of a Hong Kong public company.

The company was the first Vancouver investment dealer to become active in the International Financial Centre (IFC)—an organization made up of more than 50 banks, investment dealers, and fund managers that was formed to attract international business to the city. "We are probably one of the smallest members of the IFC, but one of the most active," says PI's Vice-

President Bob Blades, who also sits on the IFC Board.

A Commitment to the Industry

Some of British Columbia's finest financial advisers have moved to PI in recent years. They have been drawn from the more established brokerages to PI because of the company's outstanding growth, reputation, and entrepreneurial environment, as well as the opportunity to be part of a firm that encourages employee ownership.

But building a successful firm is not enough for Meier and Eymann. Both are actively involved at the executive level with the VSE and the Investment Dealers Association of Canada. "We are proud of what we give back to the industry," Meier says.

A Vision for the Future

In 1994 Marty Reynolds, a former Chairman of the VSE with extensive experience in the industry, joined PI. As the company's first Chairman, Reynolds is in charge of strategic planning, a position that Meier says has already reaped large dividends for the company. One of Reynolds' ideas was to open a Calgary office in November 1995. The firm saw the potential of the oil market, an area the company had not been involved in, and believed Alberta's political climate and lower taxes would help build the company. Next up is to open an office in Toronto and to continue the firm's penetration of institutional business through further expansion of its research and corporate finance capabilities. "We are confident we have the infrastructure in place to maintain a steady growth not only for the firm, but for our clients," Meier says.

From its new premises covering two floors in the prestigious Park Place, PI serves in excess of 30,000 clients worldwide.

THERE IS NO DOUBT THAT THE PORT OF Vancouver is an economic powerhouse in the regional economy. It creates more than 10,700 direct jobs for port workers such as longshoremen, foremen, tugboat operators, and pilots. In the summer of 1995, some of the world's largest cruise lines sailed from Vancouver to Alaska, carrying

nearly 600,000 passengers. Also during 1995 the Port handled more than 71 million tonnes of cargo—a record amount of containers, bulk, and general shipments of coal, grain, potash, sulphur, lumber, and wood pulp worth more than $30 billion.

It's a long way from 1864 when the very first ship—the *Ellen Lewis*—sailed out of Burrard Inlet, carrying lumber and fence pickets bound for Australia.

The Vancouver Port Corporation (VPC) actively administers 150 kilometres of coastal property, covering a water area of 384 square kilometres. Its jurisdiction stretches from Point Roberts at the U.S.-Canadian border, through Burrard Inlet, and includes Roberts Bank, the site of the Port's largest coal-handling facility and the future home for a state-of-the-art container terminal and grain facility.

The Port handles the third-largest amount of foreign tonnage in North America, behind south Louisiana and Houston. Vancouver is Canada's largest and most diverse port.

"The Port is meeting its competitive goals," says Vancouver Port Corporation Chairman Ron Longstaffe. "It is our aim to have shippers and shipping lines choose to use the Port of Vancouver because we offer modern facilities; excellent rail, truck, and air connections; a skilled and productive work force; commercialized terminals; favorable rates; and effective customer service programs. Vancouver has all these elements in place and we are improving them year by year."

Improvements to the infrastructure have added up to more than $300 million in recent years. "The port has made major changes and improvements to support its diversity of cargo—containers, pulp and paper, agribulk, and lumber," says Vancouver Port Corporation CEO Norman Stark. "We have done a lot to improve that structure so that the businesses using our facilities can remain competitive on a world scale and continue to grow."

The Port's two container terminals, Centerm and Vanterm, are nearing capacity and a third container terminal, Deltaport, is under construction. Deltaport is a two-berth five-crane container facility at Roberts Bank in Delta. The addition of Deltaport will more than double container capacity to more than 1 million TEUs (20-foot equivalent units). Additionally, a $175 million grain export terminal slated to open in 1999 has been proposed for the remaining site at Roberts Bank.

An increasing demand for pulp and other forest products prompted a $13 million expansion for Lynnterm, the Port's major pulp terminal. And Ballantyne Pier, the 73-year-old multipurpose terminal, received a $49 million facelift. The result is a state-of-the-art forest products facility and an attractive new cruise terminal under one roof. The Ballantyne cruise facility's original red brick façade of Shed 1 (circa 1923)

Roberts Bank, the site of the Port's largest coal-handling facility, will be the future home for a state-of-the-art container terminal and grain facility (left).

Some of the world's largest cruise lines sail to and from the Port of Vancouver at Canada Place (right).

PORT OF VANCOUVER

has been preserved as an award-winning heritage feature and will welcome passengers into the cruise industry's 14th consecutive year of growth.

Developing Relationships

The Vancouver Port Corporation sees its role as a partner with industry, labor, all levels of government, and its eight municipal neighbors. All the capital projects completed or under way have been carried out either in consultation with, or in direct partnership with, private industry. The capital and expertise for Deltaport represent a joint project between Terminal Systems Inc. (TSI), Canadian Pacific Railway Company, Canadian National Railway, and the Vancouver Port Corporation. Centerm is a partnership with the Vancouver Port Corporation and Casco Terminals, and the proposed grain terminal is a joint development with Saskatchewan Wheat Pool and Cargill Limited.

The Vancouver Port Corporation also works closely with the unions and the B.C. Maritime Employers Association (BCMEA) to ensure cooperation. A joint project that provides high-tech training for longshoremen has resulted in huge savings to business, highly trained employees, and a crane simulator and heavy equipment training centre unique to North America.

The Port is surrounded by residences, hotels, office complexes, restaurants, marinas, and parks. It is a major priority for the Vancouver Port Corporation to work cooperatively with local governments to successfully resolve issues such as pollution, movement of hazardous goods, fire protection, and property administration. "The continued good will of the adjacent eight municipalities is crucial to our operating performance and future growth," Stark says.

Making Connections

The Port's international customers come to Vancouver because it fits their criteria as a well-managed port with its stable and productive work force, the right services, and the right price. The Port of Vancouver combines leading-edge technologies with a modern and diverse infrastructure focused on the customer's needs. Location is another part of Vancouver's competitive advantage. On transpacific sailing times, Vancouver is five hours closer to Japan than Portland, 14 hours closer than Oakland, and 29 hours closer than Los Angeles. These are all crucial factors to the Port's ability to develop new business. In 1996 Hanjin and Maersk—two weekly container services—shifted their business to Vancouver. Hanjin alone represents $50 million a year to the Canadian economy.

Vancouver was the first port to open an office in Beijing. Because the Vancouver Port Corporation knows that making the right connections is vital for future business, and with more than $1.7 billion in economic benefits going to Vancouver every year, it plays a vital role in the region's future growth.

Clockwise from top left: Looking west from the Second Narrows Bridge affords a view of most of the Port's 20 major cargo and marine facilities.

Vanterm is one of the Port's two container terminals.

Each year, grain ships carry more than 10 million tonnes of grain from the Port's five grain facilities to nations worldwide.

WHEN PETER JEFFREY TOOK OVER AS PRESIDENT and Chief Executive Officer of Avcorp Industries Inc. in 1993, he inherited an aircraft parts manufacturer on the brink of extinction. Today Avcorp can boast of its strong international presence in the aerospace industry. ■ Within a year of Jeffrey's becoming President and CEO, Avcorp had taken the Canadian Productivity Award with top gold in the entrepreneurial category. The story of Avcorp had become one of innovative management practices, union co-operation, and the desire to turn an aerospace company into a global competitor.

Out of the Ashes

With divisions that had been in business for more than 40 years, Avcorp was in disastrous financial shape when Jeffrey took the reins. Each of the company's four divisions—renamed Aerostructures and Avcorp Engineering (both located in Richmond, British Columbia), Composites (Granby, Quebec), and Metal Products (Laval, Quebec)—were reorganized, two layers of management were eliminated, and a huge retraining exercise was undertaken where employees worked in teams, made decisions, and took responsibility for the outcome.

"There had been total confusion in the marketplace. Our customers were looking for one integrated supplier, so we put them all under the Avcorp banner and changed the names from their original individual corporate identities to what the divisions actually did," says Jeffrey.

Jeffrey opened the books at one division to the union's auditor and promised to increase jobs if he could squeeze out more productivity. He won a 6 percent wage rollback and, within 24 months, increased the number of jobs by 36 percent. At the same time, Avcorp implemented the Red Flag system at another division whereby any employee could raise an alarm as soon as a problem was detected. In turn, workers had more control and a stake in the outcome. Quality rose as cost savings resulted.

Building on the Red Flag system, Avcorp designed a computer system whereby clients could dial in by modem and monitor the status of any job on the shop floor. Because of its successful commitment to quality, however, Avcorp's clients have felt little need to utilize the system thus far. The system immediately caught the attention of industry giant Northrop Grumman. "The irony is," says Jeffrey, "they have never had to use the system. As soon as they got all their parts on the day we said they would and had

Peter D. Jeffrey, President and CEO (below)

Avcorp's new corporate head office is located in Richmond, British Columbia (right).

no problems with quality, there wasn't a need for them to keep checking."

Ready for the Future

As an integrated supplier—or a one-stop shop—Avcorp can design, fabricate, and assemble metal, composite, and plastic components for the aerospace industry. A significant portion of sales are from such components as the horizontal tail stabilizers for the Canadair Challenger and Regional Jet. But Avcorp also makes parts as varied as platforms for aircraft simulators, a helicopter instrument panel, or a Lockheed C-130 rudder weight assembly. In addition, Avcorp makes

doors, windows, and landing light lenses. The composite products include cabin liners, nose and tail cones, cockpit glare shields, and antennas.

In the past year, Avcorp announced a string of million-dollar contracts from companies such as Boeing, Bombardier, de Havilland Northrop Grumman, and McDonnell Douglas. Not content to rest on its numerous achievements, in 1995 the company sought and secured a design contract for putting aircraft seating in B.C. Ferries' new high-speed fleet. The company is also developing a cashierless check-out system for the U.S. market.

Diversification into areas outside aircraft parts production

is crucial for the company's survival. "The idea is to get a propriety product where we can be involved in the design and do the manufacturing, and then we will ultimately have more control over our own production," says Jeffrey. "The more that we sell of a propriety product, the more we can manufacture and set the selling price, and therefore the margins. The aerospace business is very competitive, it's global, and it's low margin unless you have a specific niche. We are working on that aspect as well."

With plants in Eastern and Western Canada, Avcorp is truly a national company, and plans through acquisitions to gain a presence in the United States. "Every country wants aerospace

Avcorp has designed and built more than 200 horizontal stabilizers and elevators (tail wings) for Canadair's Challenger Jet (top left).

Bakhshish Haylat checks the dimensions of one of the many machined parts manufactured by Avcorp as Ron Palfery, Vice President and General Manager of Avcorp's Aerostructures Division in Richmond, observes (below right).

Bill Young of the Aerostructures Division works on one of the many parts manufactured for Boeing aircraft, including the new 777 (bottom left).

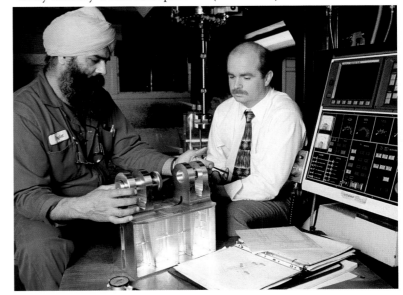

because of the quality of jobs, the skill levels, and the taxes paid. It's a labor-intensive industry," Jeffrey says.

"We have come a long way as a team, but in the end it is our customers who will determine our success. We believe that meeting customers' expectations is the price of entry. Surpassing them consistently is the formula for success," says Jeffrey. Now that Avcorp has the business of some of the world's largest aircraft manufacturers, it is the employees who will keep Avcorp competitive into the next century. By producing a smarter, streamlined company, Avcorp can compete in a global market and continue its road to success.

Fluor Daniel Wright

FLUOR DANIEL WRIGHT WAS FOUNDED IN 1988 when Fluor Daniel Inc., one of the world's leading providers of engineering, construction, and diversified services, acquired Wright Engineers Limited of Vancouver, a highly reputed engineering and construction company that had been serving the mining and metals industry since 1946. ■ Fluor Daniel Wright thereby consolidated the strengths of both companies: Wright's technical expertise and recognition in mining and metals, and Fluor Daniel's wide-ranging services, worldwide network of offices, and financial strength and reputation. With a staff of 350 located in the heart of downtown Vancouver, Fluor Daniel Wright now serves as the headquarters for the Fluor Daniel Mining & Metals Operating Company, whose other 1,400 employees are located in Denver, Colorado; Greenville, South Carolina; Santiago, Chile; Lima, Peru; Johannesburg, South Africa; and Melbourne, Australia.

Fluor Daniel has more than 50 other offices around the world, which are organized into a network of more than 30 operating companies, such as the Mining & Metals Operating Company. These companies have worked in more than 100 countries and serve more than 20 different industries, including pulp and paper, automotive, power, petrochemical, heavy industry, biotechnology and pharmaceutical, food and beverage, and telecommunications.

Fluor Corporation, the parent company, is the most diversified and broadly based engineering, construction, and diversified services company in the world, with a staff of more than 38,000. In 1995 Fluor was ranked among the top 20 of *Fortune*'s 500 most admired companies, and had sales of $8 billion and an average of 700 clients on 2,200 projects. Some of Fluor's diversified services include plant maintenance, procurement, and supplying construction equipment.

Combining these with the traditional engineering and construction services, Fluor Daniel can offer its clients nearly one-stop shopping.

With this corporate network backing it, Fluor Daniel Wright can effectively execute small and large mining and metals projects worldwide, ranging from local one-on-one consultations to the building of multibillion-dollar mines in remote regions of Canada and Latin America. It can provide feasibility studies; preliminary and detailed engineering; equipment and materials procurement; self-perform construction and construction management; and plant start-up, maintenance, and operations assistance. It applies the latest state-of-the-art techniques in estimating ore reserves and planning mine sites; designing material-handling systems, hydro- and pyrometallurgical process plants, and waste treatment systems; and providing consulting and environmental services.

"Fluor Daniel Wright has emerged as a critically important operation for the company overall," says Les McCraw, Fluor's chairman and chief executive officer. "It is the centre of our mining and metals activities worldwide, and, as such, it is the preeminent mining and metals company in the world. Some of the greatest talents in that industry reside here—truly international experts in their field."

Especially important when working in difficult terrain, SiteWorks™ software incorporates contour map data into the siting and civil works plans for mines and other facilities.

Delivering Unmatched Value

Fluor Daniel goes beyond the customary focus of an engineering and construction company. The mission of its employees is to assist clients in attaining a competitive advantage by delivering services of unmatched value.

"In today's environment, this means providing our services faster, better, cheaper, and safer," says McCraw. "We are dedicating our energies to these four goals because they are vital to our clients' success and to our ultimate aim: to be the leading diversified services company in the world."

Throughout all divisions of the company, providing quality services is the goal. Fluor Daniel believes it can provide more value to specific clients because its services are available in more geographic areas than are offered by many of its global competitors. Fluor's professionals take pride in the fact that a remarkable 80 percent of the company's business is from clients it has previously served.

Towards the Future

It is not possible to understand Fluor Daniel without addressing a philosophy the company calls Continuous Performance Improvement. In reality, it's more than a philosophy; it's an ongoing process that weaves its way through every job that every employee performs.

"We want a culture in which empowerment and entrepreneurship are encouraged and intelligent risk-taking is expected—with individual accountability as a large part of the equation," says McCraw.

Work force diversity also plays an important role in all of Fluor Daniel's offices. Each person brings a unique set of assets to the job. "Diversity makes us more client-focused, more creative, and more growth-oriented, all of which makes Fluor Daniel more competitive," says McCraw. Each project is executed

through a task force that relies upon continual teamwork between all disciplines.

"In the fast-paced industries in which we operate, maintaining the status quo can be the same as going backward," says McCraw. "Entrepreneurship, openness, innovation, responsiveness, flexibility, and teamwork must become integral to our culture. We're making progress towards changing our company culture to one that throws off outdated notions and replaces them with new ideas suited for today's environment."

To accomplish this, the company is creating an environment in which people are free to innovate, encouraged to work as a team, motivated to increase the quality of their work, and recognized for their responsiveness to client needs. In the Vancouver office, this is especially apparent. Employees enjoy the benefits of working for a small company with an open-door policy, but also are proud to work for a truly global corporation.

It is this employee dedication and adherence to the principles of client focus, innovation, and flexibility that have brought Fluor Daniel Wright to its leadership position in the industry and that will continue to serve the company well into the next century.

At the Escondida Mine in Atacama Desert, Chile, more than 200 million tons of rocks and waste material had to be excavated from the open pit to access one of the world's largest porphyritic copper orebodies 200 metres below the surface. Mining & Metals designed and built the original facility in 1990, and has worked on its three-phased expansion through 1996. The plant handles 115,000 tons of ore per day (left).

For complex plants, Fluor Daniel creates designs on microcomputers using Plant Design System™ (PDS) software, which allows multidisciplinary engineering teams to create and view complete plant systems in two or three dimensions (below).

Executing international mining projects requires archival information about similar projects and voluminous technical and socioeconomic information—drawings, standards and specifications, and articles and technical papers (left).

PAPER AND MERFIN'S AIR-LAID FABRIC HAVE only one thing in common—they are both made from wood pulp. But all similarities end there. Air-laid fabrics are softer, more absorbent, and where water is used to make paper, air is used instead in the process. "Merfin's potential is exciting. We're already manufacturing a 21st-century

product, and we're continuing to increase our production capacity to meet the world's demands," says Merfin's President and CEO Ivan B. Pivko, offering a very confident outlook. He should know. With its rapid growth—from $5 million in revenue in 1989 to an estimated $100 million in 1996—Merfin International Inc. is now a contender for the position of world market leader in air-laid specialty materials.

Formerly known as Merfin Hygienic Products Ltd., Merfin changed its corporate name in 1996 to reflect its emerging status in the international market.

Whatever You Call It. . . Don't Call It Paper.

Merfin's manufacturing process uses an innovative technology the company introduced to Canada in 1989. Air-laid fabric made by Merfin has biodegradable, yet clothlike, properties from natural wood fibres. The fibres are transported by air and laid down to form a web where either adhesive binders or a thermal bonding process is used to make

the air-laid fabric much stronger and more absorbent than paper made by the traditional wet-laid process. Furthermore, by adding super-absorbent components, air-laid fabric can be 10, 20, or even 30 times more absorbent than conventional paper.

Today Merfin distributes these fabrics internationally for use as ultrathin absorbent cores in feminine hygiene and adult incontinence products. Other important applications include hot towels, baby wipes, tabletop products, and a variety of industrial wipers.

Thanks to the use of air-laid fabric in the absorbent core, new

ultrathin superabsorbent consumer products barely resemble the bulky, uncomfortable, and leaky pads and diapers of yesteryear. The thinner, more absorbent products keep users drier and more comfortable while manufacturers deal with smaller higher-value units. Thus, shipping costs and market shelf space as well as the volume of waste sent to landfills are reduced considerably.

"We like to think of them as important lifestyle products, allowing people freedom with their normal life activities," says Pivko. "Users of this new generation of products are not

With its rapid growth, Merfin International Inc. is now a contender for the position of world market leader in air-laid specialty materials (top).

Merfin distributes air-laid fabrics internationally for use as ultrathin absorbent cores in feminine hygiene and adult incontinence products. Other important applications include hot towels, baby wipes, tabletop products, and a variety of industrial wipers (bottom).

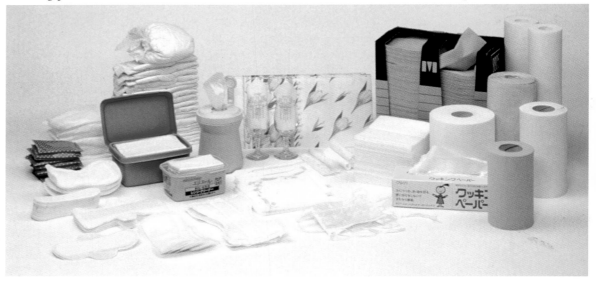

worrying about failure in their performance while working, travelling, or playing sports."

Until the 1980s, air-laid fabric was used mainly for premium table napkins in Europe and industrial wipes in North America. Advances in air-laid technology have opened new markets for personal hygiene and medical uses. In one decade, the global air-laid industry quadrupled in its size, and industry sources believe that over the next five years, annual production capacity will reach 250,000 tonnes.

Demand for this environmentally responsible product will continue to be fed by emerging economies of China, Southeast Asia, Mexico, South America, South Africa, and India. Nations from these regions have a growing middle-class ready to adopt advanced consumer products.

Merfin has come a long way since the start-up of its first air-laid machine. The company now has two air-laid production lines in its Vancouver plant—which are capable of producing up to 35,000 tonnes annually, depending on product mix—and will be adding a further 20,000 tonnes of capacity when its third machine begins production in Ireland in 1997. Additional future capacity is already being contemplated in order to keep up with the demands of the market. "Our new plant takes us closer to our European customers, the Irish labor force is

well educated, and the country has progressive tax incentives," explains Pivko.

Merfin is a key player in this emerging industry, accounting for 15 percent of worldwide production. One of just 18 air-laid manufacturers, Merfin is now the fastest-growing air-laid producer in the world.

Currently, about 85 percent of Merfin's revenue comes from its sales to world-class companies that convert air-laid fabrics into feminine and incontinence pads, baby wipes, and the hot towels used in airplanes and restaurants. Revenue of the remaining 15 percent is derived from Merfin's U.S. division, based in North Carolina. This division converts air-laid fabrics and wet-laid paper into institutional wipes, hand towels, and bathroom tissue under Merfin's trademarks: MERFIN, VICELL, PRO-NATURE, TOTE WIPES, and PERFECT WIPE PLUS.

Exports make up more than 80 percent of Merfin's business. The United States and Europe are the company's largest export markets. The Pacific Rim countries are also significant export destinations. For its outstanding export performance, Merfin has won both the Canada Export and the British Columbia Trade Export awards.

The company is listed on the Toronto Stock Exchange and the Munich Stock Exchange. Since February 1996,

Merfin has been part of the Toronto Stock Exchange's TSE 300 Composite Index. This index system is Canada's equity benchmark for the stock market performance of the most liquid, high-capitalization senior Canadian companies.

The business environment for Merfin is dominated by a major demographic shift in society. As baby boomers age and continue to influence attitudes and buying patterns, demand for thin and absorbent personal products will continue to grow. Comfort, performance, and environmentally responsible, newly developed products will further help to establish Merfin as a leader in the industry. "The opportunities for us are almost limitless as long as we continue to be innovative, internationally oriented, and niche-market focused," states Pivko.

"Merfin's potential is exciting. We're already manufacturing a 21st-century product, and we're continuing to increase our production capacity to meet the world's demands," says Merfin's President and CEO Ivan B. Pivko (above).

Merfin started the second production line in 1995, moving Merfin into the top three air-laid companies in the world, based on installed manufacturing capacity (bottom right).

Using the latest in process control technology, Merfin associates monitor all aspects of operations of its air-laid machines (bottom left).

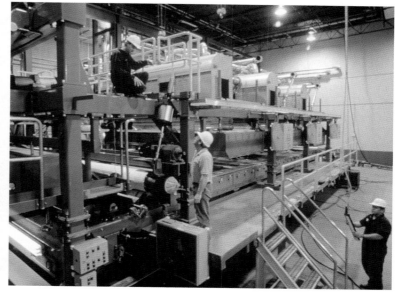

OUTSIDE THE ENTRANCE TO RICHMOND'S President Plaza a flow of water joins a dolphin and carp caught in suspended animation. The carp, a symbol of the East, and the dolphin, representing the West, illustrate the meeting of the two cultures. The water signifies life, rejuvenation, and wealth. The sculpture itself

The carp (left), a symbol of the East, and the dolphin, representing the West, illustrate the meeting of the two cultures at President Plaza.

Dr. Chin-Yen Kao (left), Chairman of President Canada Group and CEO of President Enterprises Corp., receives the prestigious President's Award—a symbol of excellence—on behalf of the Radisson President Hotel & Suites from John Norlander, President and CEO of Carlson Hospitality Worldwide, which is the parent company of Radisson Hospitality Worldwide.

is a powerful symbol of bridging the East and West. It is also the guiding philosophy behind President Canada Group (PCG), a multimillion-dollar Vancouver business empire.

The $80 million President Plaza complex—which consists of the Radisson President Hotel & Suites and the adjacent office and shopping centre—is perhaps the most visible part of PCG, a joint venture between Vancouver-based President Canada Group and one of Taiwan's largest conglomerates, President Enterprises Corp. Formed in 1989 PCG has an impressive portfolio of business holdings that include the hotel; President Chinese Restaurant; T & T Supermarkets; real estate development, management, and sales; a wholesale food-trading operation; and a range of immigration-related consultancy services.

In many ways the story behind PCG is also the story of Jack Lee, the President and driving force behind the Group. His meteoric rise from immi-grant to self-made millionaire is the stuff of legends, and his empire is a monument to what can be achieved when East and West join forces.

When East Meets West

With a degree in finance from the National Chengchi University in Taiwan and an MBA from Eastern Kentucky University in the United States, Lee found himself selling food products to Vancouver's Chinatown stores in 1978. Within two years, as demand for Asian food products rose, Lee opened Canda Enterprises Co. Ltd., which specialized in the wholesale trading of food products from Asia. In 1987 Lee needed to expand his operation. At the same time, the government of Canada introduced the immigrant-investor program to entice immigrants to invest in Canada in return for citizenship. Lee had the contacts, Canada needed the capital, and the first investment syndicate—13 investors each putting up $250,000—built a food ware-house-office building in Burnaby. This was just the beginning, and many more investment syndicates have since followed.

In 1989 Lee drew the attention of Chin-Yen Kao, the CEO of President Enter-prises Corp., a billion-dollar Taiwanese company with inter-ests that span retailing, food processing, financial services, property development, and international trading. Kao was most impressed with Lee's entre-preneurial approach and excel-lent progress in Vancouver. He also shared Lee's optimism in Canada's business potential. A joint venture partnership was formed in 1989 with the establishment of President Canada Group, for which Kao serves as Chairman.

The Building of an Empire

Lee envisioned that an increase in Asian immigration to Vancouver would create a huge demand for Asian food products and other supporting services that were essential to easing

the new immigrants into the Canadian society. "I have always believed that British Columbia is very attractive to emigrants from Asia, and it has proved to be the case in recent years," Lee says. He first turned his mind to setting up a chain of supermarkets to cater to the burgeoning Asian population.

In 1993 PCG joined forces with TAWA Supermarket Companies in the United States and opened two T & T Supermarkets in Burnaby's Metrotown Shopping Centre and Richmond's President Plaza, followed by a third one in downtown Vancouver in early 1997. T & T Supermarkets is now reckoned to be the largest Asian supermarket chain in Western Canada.

The President Chinese Restaurant, one of the finest dining establishments in the

Lower Mainland, with a seating capacity for 250 guests, opened in 1994. Its up-market dim sum dishes and seafood delicacies have been drawing diners from everywhere.

With the increase in demand for residential premises among new immigrants and others looking for investment opportunities, President Construction Inc. and President Canada Real Estate Services Inc. sprang into life in 1994, providing real estate development, management, and sales services to local and overseas customers.

While the new Open Skies policy was being discussed, Lee was building the 184-room Radisson President Hotel & Suites to meet the impending influx of visitors to the city. Five minutes from the Vancouver International Airport and 20 minutes from downtown Vancouver, the hotel—the first to carry the Radisson name in British Columbia—was poised to win the lion's share of the increased visitor traffic.

Shortly after the hotel greeted its first guests in 1994, it received the prestigious four-diamond rating from the

American Automobile Association (AAA). In 1996 the Radisson President Hotel & Suites was presented the highest honors from Radisson Hospitality Worldwide: the President's Award and the General Manager of the Year Award for its outstanding quality and service performance.

Service to the Community

Lee is a firm believer in service to the community. He is a former director of both the Richmond Chamber of Commerce and the Canada Taiwan Trade Association, past President of the Taiwan Entrepreneurs and Investors Association of British Columbia, and current Director of Tourism Vancouver. "President Canada Group owes its growth and success to Canada. We are committed to supporting the community which has helped us in so many ways," Lee says.

Vision

President Canada Group's unique strength lies in its cross-cultural corporate structure, which combines Canadian business expertise with in-depth understanding and connections in Asia. While the Group is firmly established in Canada, it maintains a strong foothold in Taiwan and other parts of Asia. By joining the best of the East and the West, Lee says, the result will always be more opportunities and prosperity for both. "We will continue to spread our wings. Our eyes are on the world."

Above: The President Plaza, an $80 million investment in Richmond, is probably the most visible part of the President Canada Group.

Middle left: Jack Lee (centre) greets guests at the Radisson President Hotel & Suites' annual Valentine's Tea Party for Seniors, which is fast becoming a Richmond tradition.

Bottom left: To support Canada's multiculturalism and promote better understanding of Chinese cultural traditions to the Greater Vancouver community, President Canada Group is one of the proud sponsors of the annual Mid-Autumn Lantern Festival. The highlight of the festivities is the Festival Lantern Parade to raise funds for United Way of the Lower Mainland in British Columbia.

Below: Dr. Chin-Yen Kao (centre), Chairman of President Canada Group, is being introduced by Jack Lee (right) to staff members of T & T Supermarket during one of Kao's visits from Taiwan.

THE OCEANSIDE COMMUNITY OF FURRY CREEK

is the West Coast's most exciting emerging community. Poised midway between Vancouver and Whistler, this master-planned community of more than 1,000 acres extends from pristine waterfront to quiet wooded mountainside lands. The final development will offer an array of

recreational choices including the spectacular Furry Creek Golf and Country Club, a marina, and hiking and biking trails on one of the most stunning waterscapes in the world. Residents of Furry Creek enjoy all the benefits of an oceanside community without the need to accommodate ferry schedules . . . close to everything and away from it all.

Furry Creek offers the ultimate in West Coast living. Breathtaking vistas of mountains and ocean abound. Secluded alpine meadows await discovery. Fresh sea and mountain air engender a sense of well-being and exhilaration. And still all the benefits of a world-class city are within easy reach. Vancouver is a mere 45 minutes away. For professional couples still commuting to the city and empty nesters enjoying the well-earned pleasures of an active lifestyle, the community opens up new worlds of discovery, both for recreational choices and natural adventure.

Displaying a strong commitment to retaining the natural setting, residences in the Oceanside Community of Furry Creek will provide unparalleled spaciousness and privacy. In order to preserve the character of the natural environment, each custom-designed home takes its inspiration from the landscape and showcases the best of coastal architecture in harmony with nature. Architectural controls also ensure that the valuable investment of each resident is protected and enhanced as the community grows. The pace and design of the development have been carefully staged to minimize impact and to ensure that the woodlands and the waterfront remain unspoiled settings for the splendid diversity of West Coast flora and fauna indigenous to the area.

In the tradition of seaside communities the world over, the heart of community life at the Oceanside Community of Furry Creek will be the Waterfront Town Centre. Anchored with a boardwalk and imbued with its own unique personality, the town centre will include a mix of multifamily and luxury lodge accommodations and meeting facilities. Cafés and bistros, art studios, and boutiques will act as a hub for visitors and residents alike to gather for fun, shopping, and socializing. Stores and services will cater to those seeking to pick up day-to-day necessities, run errands, and join in community events.

Spectacular by Nature

The waters of Howe Sound are a magnet for sailors, kayak enthusiasts, and canoeists. Scuba divers who take to the waters of nearby Porteau Cove will discover reefs and sunken ships with an abundance of marine life. Walking trips along alpine lakes and meadows provide endless photographic opportunities for capturing the wildlife, flora, and fauna of the northwest. And for those with a preference for alpine activity, there is no finer destination than Whistler Resort. Located just 60 minutes north of Furry Creek, the dual mountain ski resort offers downhill skiing, snowboarding, cross-county skiing, snowmobiling, and snowshoeing from November through March. Summer brings

Furry Creek will provide a marina for those wishing to navigate the waters of Howe Sound (near left).

The Furry Creek Golf and Country Club offers an awe-inspiring signature 14th hole on its championship golf course (far left).

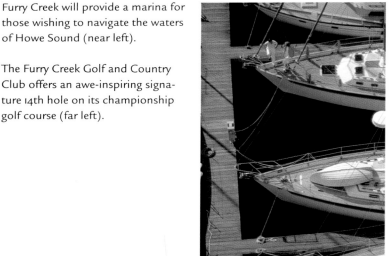

This saves passengers time and, in turn, money. "We are competing with other gateways in North America—cities like Seattle, San Francisco, and Los Angeles," explains Bruno. "We wanted to create a convenient distinctive experience for the traveller so the passengers themselves would choose to connect through Vancouver."

That's why passengers arriving in and departing from Vancouver are treated to a spectacular display. Celebrating British Columbia's inherent beauty and cultural heritage is the primary interior design theme of the International Terminal Building. From pre-eminent native artist Bill Reid's massive bronze sculpture *The Spirit of Haida Gwaii, the Jade Canoe*—located on the Departures Level—to the Musqueam art display crowned by the world's largest Coast Salish *Spindle Whorl* in the Arrivals Hall, the terminal's art presents some of the finest examples of local heritage. In addition, local contemporary artists have their work displayed on an ongoing basis throughout the terminal.

The Best of British Columbia

The West Coast theme has also been reflected in the food, beverage, and retail outlets located at the airport. When the ambience or theme of these locations was being developed, the best of British Columbia provided inspiration—Whistler Resort, Granville Island and Robson Street in Vancouver,

and the historic Steveston fishing village in Richmond.

Passengers and visitors can dine in the Pacific Market Restaurant, a delightful re-creation of Granville Island market; enjoy authentic Chinese cuisine at the Oriental Tea Garden Restaurant; or treat themselves to a myriad of fresh oysters from the Oyster Bar in the Village Square. Meanwhile, the retail offerings in the International Terminal Building have been billed as a "shopper's paradise." The diverse mix of specialty outlets—which include the Chocolate Box, Duthie Books, and Spirit of the North, to name but three of 58 shops—were all built with columns constructed from stone found in Squamish, British Columbia, and feature hardwood floors and distinctive storefronts. Internationally, nationally, and locally known outlets, as well as Allders Duty Free stores, combine to offer travellers a shopping experience they will not soon forget.

In addition to quality service and products, customers have the guarantee of fair market prices. All retailers are required to participate in the Fair Pricing Policy that ensures prices are kept in line with similar outlets in the neighboring marketplace. "Fair Pricing is absolutely fundamental," Emerson explains. "We knew that if we wanted to expand our retail revenue base, which most competitive airports want to do, we had to merchandise better and give customers value for money."

The evolution of Vancouver International Airport has produced unique exciting shops and services; mouth-watering international cuisine; and state-of-the-art technology for construction, passenger check-in facilities, air traffic control, and landing equipment, all of which are found in one of the most aesthetically pleasing airports a traveller can hope to visit. Vancouver International Airport is truly a harmonious blend of transportation, art, and culture.

Clockwise from top left:
The Pacific Market offers unique fare in a delightful atmosphere reminiscent of many of British Columbia's favorite places.

The largest Coast Salish *Spindle Whorl* "floats" from a river that flows downward between two escalators to the feet of the *Welcome Figures*.

The Village Square on the Departures Level features retail shops and restaurants to suit every taste.

PHOTOS BY DEAN SHARR—VANCOUVER INTERNATIONAL AIRPORT AUTHORITY

VANCOUVER-BASED NORAM ENGINEERING AND Constructors Ltd. has carved its own niche within the engineering industry as a supplier of world-class technology for the manufacture of key chemical products that are important to everyday living. NORAM develops and licenses process technologies and custom-designed equipment world-

NORAM supplies proprietary systems to manufacturers of chemical products, such as this mononitrobenzene plant (top left).

NORAM produces gas-to-gas heat exchangers for sulfuric acid manufacture (bottom left).

Shown here is a critical stage in the fabrication of a heat exchanger (right).

wide, supported by strong patent positions throughout Europe and the United States.

Bringing Expertise to Projects around the Globe

NORAM has made its mark internationally by supplying proprietary systems to three major business sectors: production of nitric acid, sulfuric acid, and chemicals used in the pulp and paper industries—with related bleaching process know-how. For example, NORAM has designed facilities to produce bleaching agents used to whiten wood pulp for paper production. The end products of these processes range from high-grade printing paper and letterhead to newspaper, diapers, and tissues.

NORAM is actively applying its technologies to projects in Europe, China, the United States, and Canada. Listed among its clients are some of the leading chemical producers in the world.

In the nitric acid area, NORAM has invented novel technology that is the first step in manufacturing products essential in furniture, housing insulation, footwear, and car and airplane moldings. This intermediate, mononitrobenzene, is also necessary for production of certain brand-name pharmaceuticals, agricultural formulations, and dyestuffs. The technology is currently being used by First Chemical Corporation in Pascagoula, Mississippi, and by BAYER in Antwerp, Belgium. It has been adopted also by ICI Polyurethanes at Wilton in the United Kingdom—the largest plant of its kind in the world. As an environmentally friendly system, by-product quantities are reduced to a fraction of

those formerly produced by conventional methods, a principal reason for its success and acceptance. In 1991 NORAM provided critical engineering, technical, procurement, and start-up services for A.P.'s mononitrobenzene plant in Portugal.

Among clients using NORAM's sulfuric acid technology and proprietary equipment are internationally recognizable names such as Monsanto, Rhone-Poulenc, and Phelps Dodge. These patented systems include heat exchangers, converters, and distributors, operating successfully in a business regarded as the cornerstone of the chemical manufacturing industry.

In 1993 the company purchased a substantial ownership share in B.C. Research Inc. (BCRI), which has become the research and development arm of NORAM. "Our key focus is to develop and market our own systems and technology," says Director Tom Maloney. "The acquisition of B.C. Research was an important strategic move." One of BCRI's most notable developments is a method for cloning genetically engineered softwood trees that are completely uniform, fast growing, and highly resistant to disease, providing improved management of a valuable resource.

A Partnership of Skills

Since NORAM's inception in 1982, the firm has grown from its original founders into a staff in the range of 100. The backgrounds of company principals—George Cook, Alfred Guenkel, Edward Hauptmann, John Rae, and Maloney—range from mechanical engineering to organic chemistry and are as diverse as the corporation they serve. "We brought together a variety of highly complementary skills—whether technology, marketing, or engineering," says Maloney. "We are a team. It's not an accident, it is good business and common sense."

In the future, NORAM will continue to expand its role in the chemical process technology industry. Says Maloney, "Our strategic direction will be the same: to continue to develop, refine, and acquire new technologies, and to fit carefully identified market needs."

BOB AKESTER, a native of Chilli-wack, British Columbia, moved to North Vancouver in 1970. Specializing in people, scenic, and fine art photography, he served as a set photographer for *Unforgiven*. A member of Sygma, Akester says he "would like to photograph the light of the world."

TREVOR BONDERUD, who resides in Victoria, is originally from Kamloops, British Columbia. Specializing in people and conceptual photography, Bonderud is married and has two children.

ROGER BROOKS, whose areas of specialty include architectural and interior photography, won the 1993 gold medal in the Artistes Français Exhibition in Paris. A native of England, Brooks earned a bachelor of science in civil engineering and currently resides in Vancouver. He enjoys travelling with his family and took a year off to travel in France in 1993.

DAVID COOPER, owner and operator of David Cooper Photography, was born in Toronto. Moving to Vancouver in 1975, he specializes in photographing the performing arts, including theatre, dance, and music. Cooper's client list includes the Stratford Festival Theatre, Oregon Shakespeare Festival, Ballet British Columbia, Royal Winnipeg Ballet, and Vancouver Opera. His work with the Shaw Festival Theatre, for which he has served as company photographer since 1980, earned Cooper a bronze medal in advertising from the Canadian Association of Photographers and Illustrators in Communications (CAPIC).

STAN CZOLOWSKI, born and raised in Vancouver, is a free-lance photographer who specializes in images of the West Coast as well as historic and botanical photography. His work can be seen in *Vancouver* magazine, *Georgia Straight*, *The World of Stanley Park*, *Songs of the Wild*, and *Trialogues at the Edge of the West*. For

years Czolowski shot production stills for local television stations and produced audiovisual slide video pieces dealing with myth and magic.

ED GIFFORD, a graduate of the University of New Mexico, studied photography under Beaumont Newhall before immigrating to Vancouver in 1974 and pursuing a free-lance photography career. Gifford developed a photography division within the Richmond Adult Education Department, offering a full curricu-

▲ FRED HERZOG

lum to more than 200 students. Also teaching through the University of British Columbia (UBC) Continuing Education Department, Emily Carr Institute of Art and Design, and Camera Canada College, he was the codirector of CREO3, a nonprofit gallery and school in Vancouver.

DOANE GREGORY, originally from New York, moved to Vancouver in 1982. The recipient of a bachelor's degree in comparative religion from Colorado State University, he specializes in magazine editorial, celebrity, and travel/stock photography. Gregory has won the Communication Arts Award of Excellence twice, was a finalist in the New York Art Director's Festival, and has won two awards of excellence from the Graphic Designers of Canada. In addition to being featured in such publications as *Playback*, *Photo Life*,

and *Photo District News*, he has done work for such companies as IBM, Eastman Kodak, and Vancouver Opera.

GREG GRIFFITH is a native of New Zealand who moved to Whistler, British Columbia, 20 years ago. Employed by Mountain Monuments Photography, Griffith specializes in photographing such subjects as skiing and mountains.

ANNIE GRIFFITHS-BELT specializes in photojournalism and is widely

▲ FRED HERZOG

published. She photographed Vancouver while on assignment for *National Geographic* in 1991. Griffiths-Belt lives in Washington, D.C., with her husband and daughter.

KIKU HAWKES specializes in people and fashion, architectural and landscape, and editorial photography, as well as hand-coloring and alternative processes. Having exhibited her work across Canada, Hawkes has won awards from Canada Council, CAPIC, Canadian Broadcasting Corporation, and the National Film Board. A native of Germany, Hawkes studied at Friends World College and Emily Carr Institute of Art and Design.

CHRIS HARRIS, who lives in One Hundred Mile House, British Columbia, is originally from Montreal. A teacher and mountain guide,

Harris specializes in the subject of British Columbia.

BRENDA HEMSING's areas of specialty include fine art and landscape photography and photojournalism. Among her favorite subjects are forests, mountains, and ocean scenes. She has contributed to the ArtBank of Canada, Washington State Arts Commission, Air Canada, and Alberta Culture Provincial Archives collections, as well as to *Gallerie* magazine and *Camera Canada*.

FRED HERZOG, a native of Germany, moved to Vancouver in 1953. The owner and operator of Fred Herzog Photography, he specializes in urban documentation and kinesics. The recipient of a Canada Council grant in 1969, he participated in a three-man show, *Extensions*, which travelled across the country under the auspices of the National Gallery of Canada. Herzog has contributed to such books as *The City of Vancouver* and *Vancouver: Vision of a City*.

KENT KALLBERG, born and raised in Vancouver, is a self-taught photographer who specializes in being a generalist. His clients include Orca Bay Sports and Entertainment, Westin Bayshore, *Sports Illustrated*, LaBatt's, McDonald's, Palmer Jarvis Advertising, and Vancouver International Airport. A professional broadcaster for 13 years, Kallberg runs Kallberg Darch Studios Ltd.

ROBERT KARPA specializes in editorial portraiture and considers Bryan Adams, Arthur Erickson, and Arthur Griffiths to be some of his favorite subjects to photograph. Karpa's work can be seen in such magazines as *Rolling Stone*, *LA Style*, *Seventeen*, *Forbes*, *Fortune*, and *Money*. He has won many awards, including two Gold Awards for his editorial portraits—one from *Canada* magazine and one from the Toronto Art Director's Club. Originally from Cambridge, Ontario, Karpa moved to Vancouver in 1970. He holds a bachelor's degree in marine biology.

THOMAS KITCHIN is a self-employed photographer who specializes in

wildlife images. Having lived all over, he has a degree in recreation/social work. Kitchin works with his wife and partner, Victoria Hurst.

ROB KRUYT, who earned a professional photography diploma from the Western Academy of Photography in Victoria, is an editorial and commercial photographer who moved to Vancouver in 1990. Specializing in people, places, and events, Kruyt has been a regular contributor to most of Vancouver's magazines and newspapers. In 1995 he participated in a solo exhibition, *Art in Public Spaces*, at the Hong Kong Bank Atrium and Queen Elizabeth Theatre Gallery. Kruyt has also contributed images to *Great Work! An Overview of Contemporary British Columbia Artists*.

ROBERT KWONG, a member of Professional Photographers of Canada, specializes in action sports, motorsports, people and events, and aerial photography. His clients include Molson Indy, Molson Thunderfest, Tourism Canada, National Dairy Council, and Chevron Oil. A native of Vancouver, Kwong is an avid downhill skier and mountain biker, and enjoys riding his Harley Davidson.

KEVIN McGOWAN, originally from Milwaukee, is a commercial photographer for Strode Photographers where he specializes in food, product, industrial, and architectural assignments. McGowan's work has been displayed in the Everson Musuem of Art in Syracuse, New York, and he has received awards from the Professional Photographers Association of Washington for his commercial photography. Previous clients include the Roman Meal Company, STL International, and the American Plywood Association. McGowan particularly enjoys shooting travel, nature, and lifestyle images. He spends his leisure time hiking, camping, and playing guitar.

PATRICK MORROW, a native of Kimberley, British Columbia, is a self-taught photographer who has won many awards for his work in photography and video. He works extensively for *Equinox* magazine.

An avid mountaineer, Morrow is listed in the *Guinness Book of World Records* as the first person to climb the highest peaks on all seven continents and the first Canadian to climb Mount Everest.

DAVID NANUK is a self-employed photographer whose areas of specialty include the West Coast of British Columbia and astronomy. A resident of Aldergrove, British Columbia, Nanuk earned a bachelor of science from UBC.

YUKIKO ONLEY, who was raised and educated in Japan, moved to Vancouver in 1976. An equestrienne who photographs horses and riders, Onley also specializes in fine art and travel photography.

JOHN T. PENNINGTON, a native of Toronto, currently resides in Vancouver and is the operator of Sea-Pen Photographic. Pennington specializes in underwater photography in the Pacific Northwest and British Columbia, and his work can be seen in *Dive Training*, *Canada Geographic*, *Photo Life*, and *Discover Diving* magazines.

ART PERRY, a resident of Vancouver, attended Carleton University and UBC. Specializing in documentary photography, Perry has worked for such publications as *Vancouver*, *Step*, *Georgia Straight*, *San Francisco Focus*, *Pacific Report*, and *Canadian Art*.

DAVID PRICHARD is a well-travelled stock photographer who has spent much of his time photographing Vancouver's mountains. Prichard lives in Toronto.

JASON PUDDIFOOT is a self-employed photographer whose areas of specialty include outdoor, nature, and underwater photography and panoramics. His work can be seen in *National Geographic*. Born and raised in Vancouver, Puddifoot includes bears among his favorite subjects.

STEFAN SCHULHOF, a member of Professional Photographers' Association of British Columbia, Professional Photographers of Canada, and CAPIC, is an award-

ADANAC CUSTOMS BROKERS LTD. 168
AIRBC 212
ALLIANCE MERCANTILE INC. 178
AVCORP INDUSTRIES INC. 218
AXA PACIFIC INSURANCE COMPANY 210
BCTV. 180
BLAIKLOCK INC. 206
CANADIAN AIRLINES INTERNATIONAL LTD. 164
CANADIAN NATIONAL RAILWAY COMPANY 163
CANADIAN PACIFIC RAILWAY COMPANY—CANADIAN PACIFIC HOTELS—
    MARATHON REALTY COMPANY LIMITED 148
CAPILANO COLLEGE. 196
THE CERTIFIED GENERAL ACCOUNTANTS' ASSOCIATION OF CANADA. 200
COMMONWEALTH INSURANCE COMPANY. 186
DOMINION BLUEPRINT & REPROGRAPHICS LTD. 162
EBCO INDUSTRIES LTD. 174
FINNING LTD. 166
FLUOR DANIEL WRIGHT 220
GROUP WEST SYSTEMS LTD. 208
IMPERIAL PARKING LIMITED 184
ISM-BC INFORMATION SYSTEMS MANAGEMENT 230
JARDINE INSURANCE SERVICES CANADA. 156
MCCARTHY TÉTRAULT 182
MCDONALD'S RESTAURANTS OF CANADA LIMITED. 190
MERFIN INTERNATIONAL INC. 222
MOLI ENERGY (1990) LIMITED 228
MURCHIE'S TEA & COFFEE LTD. 152
NORAM ENGINEERING AND CONSTRUCTORS LTD. 234
C.M. OLIVER 158
PACIFIC INTERNATIONAL SECURITIES INC. 214
PALMER JARVIS ADVERTISING 202
PITMAN BUSINESS COLLEGE 154
PRESIDENT CANADA GROUP 224
SEABOARD NORTH AMERICAN HOLDINGS, INC. 172
SERVICE CORPORATION INTERNATIONAL (CANADA) LIMITED 198
SHATO HOLDINGS LTD. 204
H.A. SIMONS LTD. 170
TANAC DEVELOPMENT CANADA CORPORATION 226
TCG INTERNATIONAL INC. 192
VANCOUVER BOARD OF TRADE 150
VANCOUVER INTERNATIONAL AIRPORT. 232
VANCOUVER PORT CORPORATION 216
VANCOUVER STOCK EXCHANGE 160